On Story—Screenwriters and Their Craft

On Story

Screenwriters and Their Craft

AUSTIN FILM FESTIVAL

EDITED BY

Barbara Morgan AND *Maya Perez*

UNIVERSITY OF TEXAS PRESS ⋎ AUSTIN

Requests for permission to reproduce material
from this work should be sent to:
Permissions
University of Texas Press
P.O. Box 7819
Austin, TX 78713-7819
http://utpress.utexas.edu/index.php/rp-form

Design by Lindsay Starr

The paper used in this book meets the minimum requirements
of ANSI/NISO Z39.48-1992 (R1997) (Permanence of Paper). ∞

Library of Congress Cataloging-in-Publication Data

On story : screenwriters and their craft /
edited by Barbara Morgan and Maya Perez. — First edition.
pages   cm
ISBN 978-0-292-75460-7 (pbk. : alk. paper)
1. Screenwriters—Interviews. 2. Motion picture authorship.
3. On story: presented by Austin Film Festival (Television program)
I. Morgan, Barbara, 1962–, editor of compilation. II. Perez, Maya, 1970–,
editor of compilation. III. Austin Film Festival.
PN1996.O5 2013
808.2'3—dc23
2013008525

doi:10.7560/754607

Dedicated to

Frank Pierson, Polly Platt, Sydney Pollack,
and Bud Shrake

Contents

Foreword

Is screenwriting an art or a craft? I really don't give a rat's ass. A story's a story. A movie's a movie. I want the end product, not how it got there. The truth is, the Pope gave Michelangelo notes on the Sistine Chapel. The truth is, the ceiling's centerpiece, the creation of Adam, is not even an original idea. Old Mike Angelo adapted it from a scene in Genesis. The truth is, it was a work for hire.

Another truth is that there are some people who want to believe the world is a scam, a place where if you can just work out the game, everything falls into place. Read this book. Read between its lines, and do you know what you'll learn? There is no shortcut to excellence; there is no trick to writing a movie. It is hard work. The sacrifice involved is daunting; the dues you must pay are monumental. That's what Frank Pierson and John Lee Hancock know. You get to where you want to be by getting there. You want to play baseball? Don't show up in the Bronx and tell them you're ready to play shortstop for the New York Yankees. Go to a sandlot with a bat, a glove, and a ball. Carnegie Hall? Practice, baby, practice. Go on. You might have the time of your life along the way.

I personally am uncomfortable with the title of writer. I am a filmmaker. I make movies. Watching them as a boy made me realize there was a world out there. Movies altered my horizon. As an adult, movies have put me in a solitary cell for months at a time. They have taken me around the world literally and figuratively. They've introduced me to my greatest friends and my most mortal enemies. They sprung me from my childhood purgatory and gave me my life, and I am inescapably in their debt.

Despite signing away said life to them, I don't have a lot of rules about movies or the writing of screenplays. I just have a few things I know. First and maybe last, it never gets easier. If it does, you are probably doing it badly. Writing a screenplay is like digging the Panama Canal from one end of your brain to the other. It takes about two thousand hours. Put an inordinate amount of time into one end and a screenplay comes out the other.

It is a lonely task. And if it is not sometimes unbearably lonely, you are doing it wrong.

Having chosen this path, you must never stop. My first representation was at an agency so low-rent they could not afford to make photocopies. Every time I wrote a new script, I had to drop off ten copies. Six unsold scripts later, I received a call: "Your work is taking up too much space." What that meant wasn't exactly clear until two hours later when I was staggering down Sunset Boulevard with dozens of copies of my unsold screenplays in my arms. Rock bottom is where you need to get to. It's where most of the people in this book have ended up at one time or another. Rock bottom is where you begin. The first screenplay I sold was the seventh I wrote. Had I given up, I wouldn't be typing this foreword today.

That's about all I have to say. There may be common knowledge, but each writer sees the world through his or her own prism. That is essential, because movies are subjective. Never mind the audience as a whole; the power of a movie lies in how it can affect one single person. Like a tornado careening past—touching one, leaving another unscathed. Screenwriting is subjective as well. So are the writers in this book. Thank God. And as they crisscross a lonely desert, Austin is an oasis, unique in that it knows something no one else can seem to remember—the script is the star. Despite my battle-scarred skepticism of this world, I do not disagree.

Brian Helgeland
Pt. Dume, California
November 3, 2012

Acknowledgments

On Story is a compilation of two decades dedicated to the celebration of the art and craft of storytelling. Since its creation in 1993, Austin Film Festival has continuously focused on the writers' contributions to film by recognizing and championing the work of the writer as the core of the creative process in filmmaking. This book highlights the natural progression of Austin Film Festival's mission, and for that we owe a huge debt of gratitude to those who, throughout the years, have made our vision possible.

First and foremost, this book came to fruition due to the contribution, support, and collaboration from the following distinguished screenwriters: John August, Sacha Gervasi, John Lee Hancock, Peter Hedges, Brian Helgeland, Lawrence Kasdan, Nicholas Kazan, Daniel Petrie Jr., Frank Pierson, Anne Rapp, Bud Shrake, Whit Stillman, Robin Swicord, Caroline Thompson, Randall Wallace, Bill Wittliff, and Steven Zaillian. These screenwriters have been active participants in our annual Conference, and we thank them for sharing their rich and personal stories.

We are thankful to the University of Texas Press, more specifically Jim Burr, Nancy Bryan, Victoria Davis, Lynne Chapman, Molly Frisinger, and Kaila Wyllys, for their support and assistance in putting this book together. We thank Deena Kalai, Esq., for her legal guidance in the completion of this book.

Thank you to the following individuals, without whose dedicated attention and support this book would not have been written: Erin Hallagan, Miguel Alvarez, Colter Baldwin, Linzy Beltran, Allison Frady, Jardine Libaire, Samantha Rae Lopez, Marcelena Mayhorn, Sonia Onescu, and Alison Week.

In addition, we thank all those who have championed and supported Austin Film Festival over the past twenty years—attendees, panelists, filmmakers, moderators, staff interns, transcribers, volunteers, Fred Miller, and Austin Film Festival board members Shane Black, Barry Josephson, and Marsha Milam. We are forever grateful to the late, great Mary Margaret Farabee, as her kindness, generosity, and endless support helped make this book happen. We would also like to give a special thanks to Allen Odom for his dedicated effort and attention to this book. Further, we would like to thank Keith Carter for allowing us to use his photograph to represent our book.

Finally, we extend our gratitude and appreciation to those close friends and family members whose boundless love and support was the driving force behind the making of this book.

Screenwriter Biographies

John August's screenwriting credits include *Go*, *Charlie and the Chocolate Factory*, *Big Fish*, and *Frankenweenie*. He wrote and directed *The Nines* and has created pilots for Fox and ABC, as well as the series *D.C.* for The WB. August is also an app developer, having developed FDX Reader for iPhones/iPads and Bronson Watermarker for Macintosh. August's popular websites http://johnaugust.com/ and http://screenwriting.io/ provide information for aspiring screenwriters.

Sacha Gervasi is a British journalist, screenwriter, and director whose film-writing credits include *The Big Tease*, which he co-wrote with Craig Ferguson; *The Terminal*, directed by Steven Spielberg; and *Henry's Crime*, which he also executive produced. His directing credits include the Academy–Award nominated *Hitchcock*, starring Anthony Hopkins, Helen Mirren, and Scarlett Johansson, and the documentary *Anvil! The Story of Anvil*, for which he won an Independent Spirit Award and an Emmy Award.

John Lee Hancock's breakthrough as a major player came when he scripted Clint Eastwood's *A Perfect World*, and he reteamed with Eastwood for the screen version of *Midnight in the Garden of Good and Evil*, adapting the best-selling book by John Berendt. Hancock is a credited writer on *Snow White and the Huntsman*, wrote and directed *The Alamo* and *The Blind Side*, and directed *The Rookie* as well as the upcoming *Saving Mr. Banks*.

Peter Hedges is a playwright, novelist, screenwriter, and director. He wrote both the novel and the screenplay for *What's Eating Gilbert Grape* and co-wrote *About a Boy*, for which he received an Academy Award nomination. As writer-director, his films include *Pieces of April*, *Dan in Real Life*, and *The Odd Life of Timothy Green*.

Brian Helgeland is a critically acclaimed writer, producer, and director. His screenwriting credits include *L.A. Confidential*, for which he received an Academy Award for Best Adapted Screenplay, *Mystic River*, *A Nightmare on Elm Street 4: The Dream Master*, and *Payback*. Helgeland also wrote and directed the films *42*, *A Knight's Tale,* and *The Order*, as well as helped co-write *The Bourne Supremacy*.

Lawrence Kasdan, a four-time Academy Award nominee, has directed eleven films, among them *Body Heat*, *The Big Chill*, *The Accidental Tourist*, *Wyatt Earp*, *Dreamcatcher*, *Grand Canyon*, and *Darling Companion*, the last two co-written with his wife, Meg Kasdan. He has written or co-written four of the most successful films in history: *Raiders of the Lost Ark*, *The Empire Strikes Back*, *Return of the Jedi*, and *The Bodyguard*.

Nicholas Kazan is a critically acclaimed playwright, writer, producer, and director. He has penned screenplays for films including *At Close Range*, *Fallen*, and *Bicentennial Man*, as well as *Reversal of Fortune*, which was nominated for an Academy Award for Best Adapted Screenplay. With his wife, Robin Swicord, he co-wrote *Matilda*, adapted from the beloved Roald Dahl novel. He is the director of *Dream Lover*.

Daniel Petrie Jr.'s screenwriting credits include *Beverly Hills Cop*, for which he was nominated for an Academy Award, *The Big Easy*, *Shoot to Kill*, and *Turner & Hooch*. He is the writer and director of *Toy Soldiers*, *In the Army Now*, and several films made for television, including *Framed*. Petrie was the co-creator, showrunner, and executive producer of the series *Combat Hospital*. He served two terms as president of the Writers Guild of America, West.

Frank Pierson (1925–2012) was a prolific screenwriter whose credits include *Cat Ballou*, *Cool Hand Luke*, and *Dog Day Afternoon*, for which he won an Academy Award. Pierson wrote and directed *A Star Is Born*, *Somebody Has to Shoot the Picture*, and *Conspiracy*, among others. He was twice president of the Writers Guild of America, West, as well as president of the Academy of Motion Picture Arts and Sciences.

Anne Rapp began her screenwriting career with *Cookie's Fortune* and *Dr. T and the Women*, both produced and directed by Robert Altman. She has written for *Gun*, an ABC series, and she wrote *Stars Over Texas*, a CMT special starring Dolly Parton. Rapp, also a short story writer and essayist, is currently directing and producing a documentary about acclaimed playwright and screenwriter Horton Foote.

Bud Shrake (1931–2009) wrote the screenplays for *J.W. Coop*, *Kid Blue*, *Nightwing*, *Tom Horn*, and *Songwriter*. In addition, he co-wrote *Pair of Aces* and *Another Pair of Aces: Three of a Kind*. Shrake was also a critically acclaimed novelist, essayist, and biographer whose literary archives are held by the Southwestern Writers Collection at Texas State University–San Marcos.

Whit Stillman is the writer-director of *Barcelona*, *The Last Days of Disco*, *Damsels in Distress*, and *Metropolitan*, for which he received an Academy Award nomination for Best Original Screenplay. Stillman also published a novelization of *The Last Days of Disco* entitled *The Last Days of Disco, with Cocktails at Petrossian Afterwards*.

Robin Swicord's screenwriting credits include *Memoirs of a Geisha*, *Little Women*, *Matilda* (which she wrote and produced with Nicholas Kazan), and *The Curious Case of Benjamin Button*, for which she received an Academy Award nomination. She also wrote two Off-Broadway plays, *Last Days at the Dixie Girl Café* and *Criminal Minds*. Swicord adapted and directed *The Jane Austen Book Club* and is currently adapting an E. L. Doctorow short story, "Wakefield."

Caroline Thompson is the writer of *Edward Scissorhands*, *The Addams Family*, *Homeward Bound: The Incredible Journey*, *The Secret Garden*, *The Nightmare Before Christmas*, *Corpse Bride*, and *City of Ember*. She is also the writer and director of *Black Beauty*, *Buddy*, and *Snow White: The Fairest of Them All*. Thompson is currently at work on adaptations of Melissa Marr's Young Adult novel *Wicked Lovely* and Mikhail Bulgakov's masterpiece, *The Master and Margarita*. In addition, she is writing *Marwencol* for Robert Zemeckis, based on the documentary of the same name, and adapting George Orwell's *Animal Farm*.

Randall Wallace's film credits include *Pearl Harbor*, *We Were Soldiers*, *The Man in the Iron Mask*, *Secretariat*, and *Braveheart*, for which he received an Academy Award nomination, a Golden Globe nomination, and the Writers Guild of America Award for Best Original Screenplay. Mr. Wallace is also a novelist, a lyricist, and the founder of Wheelhouse Entertainment, an independent entertainment company.

Bill Wittliff's screenwriting and producing credits include *The Perfect Storm*, *The Black Stallion*, and *Legends of the Fall*, as well as *Lonesome Dove*, for which he won a Writers Guild of America Award. His photography has been published in *Vaquero: Genesis of the Texas Cowboy*, *La Vida Brinca: A Book of Tragaluz Photographs*, and most recently, *A Book of Photographs from Lonesome Dove*.

Steven Zaillian has written many critically acclaimed films, including *The Girl With the Dragon Tattoo*, *Awakenings*, *American Gangster*, and *Schindler's List*, which won an Academy Award for Best Adapted Screenplay. Zaillian co-wrote *Moneyball* and *Gangs of New York*, both nominated for Academy Awards, and he is the writer-director of *Searching for Bobby Fischer*, *A Civil Action*, and *All the King's Men*.

Please note: Unless otherwise stated, all credits in the book are writing credits.

On Story—Screenwriters and Their Craft

Introduction

Stories are elemental to our species. Almost as basic as light, shelter, food, or water. We've needed them from the very start of humanity as a way of connecting our lives, as a way of sustaining, provoking, and even saving one another. And the way we communicate stories has evolved with our technological abilities. Whether they tell tales with blood on cave walls, with the typewritten word, or with digital images, storytellers are instigators and guardians of the compassion vital to survival.

As a collaborative medium, film is a unique form, fusing the ideas and imaginations of a slew of contributors into one entity. Sometimes films can seem to tumble out of the grand subconscious without any specific author to credit, but movies generally begin in one mind. This book is about the moment a film is born and how it evolves, told from the perspective of its originator—the storyteller.

There are infinite ways to create a story, and this volume of *On Story* is less interested in dictating them than in cataloguing the diverse experiences and insights of this era's great auteurs. The advice inside will be contradictory, genuine, and kinetic, and the desired result is singular—to arrive at that feeling when the lights go down and we lose ourselves to a great story.

Founded in 1993, Austin Film Festival was the first organization of its kind to focus on the writer's creative contribution to film. Originally the Heart of Film Screenwriters Conference, a forum for craft development, inspiration, networking, and career launching, AFF still hinges on the screenwriter and has since grown to serve filmmakers, too.

When we began, we didn't know we were filling a gaping hole in the landscape; writers simply didn't have an outlet for convening and for discussion and development. We weren't sure we'd have the audience to sustain this creator-based venture, but soon enough found that not only was the audience there, but it was receptive and wanting to be inspired.

We're still here, growing exponentially every year, and solidifying a reputation as one of the most exciting idea exchanges in the country. It turns out most writers and creators working in cerebral solitude don't mind the chance to mingle, collaborate, and compare notes with their peers once a year—how lucky we are!

The Film Festival and Conference offers more than 200 films, and 90 panels, workshops, and roundtable discussions led by over 150 industry professionals. Due to AFF's devotion to creators and to story, we're recognized and known as a one-of-a-kind open and productive summit. Veterans are refreshed by new ideas and old friends, and newcomers emerge with mentors as well as advice and insight from masters.

Besides an annual Film Festival and Conference, AFF hosts a wealth of year-round screenings and discussions, and without even knowing how valuable and illuminating the end results would be, we had the notion to record every panel, conversation, and presentation from AFF's beginning. With over nineteen years now of high-caliber artists talking candidly and provocatively about their work and about the art and craft of screenwriting and filmmaking in general, we've decided to cull the cream of the footage and make it available to the public.

The resulting multitiered On Story Project includes AFF's TV show called *On Story*, curated from this footage of AFF discussions, presentations, and Q&A's, and currently airing on many PBS-affiliated stations and streaming online; the companion book set, also called *On Story*, of which this is the first volume; the *On Story* archive, the digital preservation of these decades of AFF footage, which will be donated to and housed and disseminated by the Wittliff Collections at Texas State University; and an interactive *On Story* website where one can read more transcripts, watch short films and *On Story* episodes, communicate with other writers, filmmakers, and fans, and check out more footage of talks and presentations (at www.onstory.tv).

Candor and generosity inform the culture at AFF. Because our screenings, panel discussions, and presentations celebrate creativity and storytelling, we have an outstanding array of artists who loyally and happily participate every year—and we are grateful to them all.

The phenomenal list of AFF participants over two decades has included: Robert Altman (*Nashville*), Wes Anderson and Owen Wilson (*Rushmore*), Robert Benton (*Bonnie and Clyde*), James L. Brooks (*Terms of Endearment*), Joel and Ethan Coen (*Fargo*), Johnny Depp (*Pirates of the Caribbean*), Lindsay Doran (*Sense and Sensibility*), Robert Duvall (*The Godfather*), Ted Elliott and Terry Rossio (*Shrek*), Horton Foote (*To Kill a Mockingbird*), James Franco (*Sal*), Pamela Gray (*Conviction*), Buck Henry (*The Graduate*), Lawrence Kasdan (*Body Heat*), John Lasseter (*Toy Story*), Barry Levinson (*Rain Man*), Alexander Payne and Jim Taylor (*Sideways*), Frank Pierson (*Cool Hand Luke*), Sydney Pollack (*Out of Africa*), Harold Ramis (*Groundhog Day*), Paul Schrader (*Taxi Driver*), Whit Stillman (*Metropolitan*), Oliver Stone (*Platoon*), Caroline Thompson (*Edward Scissorhands*), Robert Towne (*Chinatown*), Chris and Paul Weitz (*About a Boy*), and Steven Zaillian (*Schindler's List*).

Film used to be an exclusive, expensive medium. These days, you can make a film with affordable, bare-bones equipment. The art form is wide open. The *On Story* show, the *On Story* books, the *On Story* website, and the *On Story* archive offer an unparalleled range of lessons on the art and craft of screenwriting and filmmaking—to professionals, and to any curious newcomer who wants to take a shot. *Los Angeles Times* film critic Kenneth Turan said about the TV show: "*On Story* is film school in a box, a lifetime's worth of filmmaking knowledge squeezed into half-hour packages." So enjoy this collection of ideas, use it in your own way, and remember that the only place to begin a journey is inspiration.

Barbara Morgan
Austin Film Festival Cofounder
and Executive Director

1

Inspiration

A Conversation with
Randall Wallace

I grew up in Tennessee. My father is from Lizard Lick, Tennessee. The men in my family are Alton, Elton, Dalton, Lionel, Herman, Thurman, and Clyde. They call Clyde "Pete," but no one has any idea why. I don't know where y'all are from, but I don't think it could be more down-to-earth than Lizard Lick, so I'm one of y'all.

I always thought it was funny when I was trying to figure out how I was going to get anywhere and get anybody to read anything. I felt there was this enormous gulf between where I was and where they were. When I was in college—I think I might have been in graduate school—one of my professors said to me, "If you want to be a lawyer, I can show you the bottom rung of the ladder. When you get a hold of that bottom rung, if you can pull yourself up, the next rung will be within your reach. That's how you climb the ladder and become a lawyer. If you want to be a doctor, I can show you that, but to be a writer . . . I don't know where that ladder is." But there is one. It's like the metaphor of dropping into the deep, dark woods and being lost. When you're in the woods for a while, you become an expert in woodcraft, you learn where to find water, you learn how to build a fire, you learn where to find shelter, you learn where it's dangerous. You're following your instincts.

I think that's the gulf—if there is one—between you and me, and that's the gulf I'm here to help break down. I've been in the woods a bit longer, but it's the same woods we're in together. We have similar needs, and in similar ways we're searching.

The Origins of *Braveheart*

I had married an amazing Irish-American woman. I always said if you threw her into a barrel of cobras, she would come out with a purse. I wanted to have children, and she wasn't sure she did. She said, "If you get me pregnant, you have to take me to Europe," which was her favorite thing, so I said, "Okay."

She knew all about her family history because she had Mormon ancestors, and they knew everything about where they were from. I was your basic Southerner; I had no ethnic identity. We were just Americans. I didn't actually know until later that that is characteristic of the Scots-Irish, that immediately getting off the boat, they all said, "We're Americans." That's why you didn't have a hyphen. You don't hear "Scottish-American." My family came to America in the 1660s. I don't know why we didn't buy real estate.

I wanted to know what my family's heritage was in the context of being a soon-to-be father, so we went to Edinburgh, Scotland. I'd heard that the Wallaces were from Scotland. At that time, I had been a songwriter and had been so successful at that that I decided to write screenplays. I wasn't getting anywhere with anything. I had sold a few things and had a couple of novels that had taken me a year to write apiece, and I had made about $5,000, so I would have qualified for welfare. But we were frugal and had saved our money, so we could buy the plane tickets.

In Edinburgh Castle, flanking the main door into the castle, were two statues—"William Wallace" and "Robert the Bruce." I had never heard of William Wallace. I had heard of Robert the Bruce, the greatest king of Scotland. If William Wallace is standing there with him, he must have been good. So I asked—there was a member of the Black Watch Guards . . . Does anyone in this room have a kilt? I will tell you, if you put a kilt on, you will become a bad mo-fo. You just walk around and look at guys going, "What'd you say? What?" because you've got on a skirt, right? Excuse my French, but that's how you feel. This guy is standing there in a kilt, and I said, "Who is this William Wallace?" And he said, "He is our greatest hero." I was absolutely fascinated by history, and here is this man named Wallace who is standing next to Robert the Bruce, and the guard's saying William Wallace is the greatest hero. And I had never heard of him. And my name is Wallace. And that alone just made me think, "What?"

I, of course, am with my pregnant wife going, "Greatest hero . . . Greatest hero . . ." So I said to the guy, "He must have been an ally of Robert the Bruce and fought the English," because I knew that's what Robert the Bruce had done. He said, "No one will ever know for sure." By the way, those are the magic words for a screenwriter, "No one will ever know for sure." He said, "Legends say that Robert the Bruce may have been one of William Wallace's betrayers to clear the way for him to become king." I nearly fell down. I thought, "That's like being told that Judas Iscariot and St. Peter were the same individual, that the man who betrayed the greatest hero then became the greatest king. What if . . . ?" And that's another great question of the screenwriter, "What if . . . ?" What if something about the life and death of William Wallace was what transformed Robert the Bruce from being the kind of man who would betray a hero to the kind of man who would become a great king himself? That felt like a magnificent question.

> Those are the magic words for a screenwriter, "No one will ever know for sure."

My wife was pregnant, I didn't have any money, and it was ten years before I would sit down and tell the story, but I'll tell you now, the trials and tribulations. Forgive me for making this too personal. My route is not a map you can follow, but what my route is, I think, is an endorsement of your route. I believe when you're a writer, you're following a light. It is, in fact, divine. I cuss once in a while so I don't sound too much like a Baptist preacher, which is what I wanted to be and still sometimes do, but I think it's a calling. I will not let two things stop me: One is fear of failure, and the other is lack of effort. Those two things will never stop me. That was my commitment. I don't know if I had the talent, the luck, or whatever the combination of ingredients; I was never going to be afraid to be rejected— not enough to stop me—and I was never going to not try enough.

> I will not let two things stop me: One is fear of failure, and the other is lack of effort.

I started working, I ended up in television, I had a lot of money, things were working really well, and then we had the writers' strike. By the way, every time we strike, it is a disaster. To strike is to go to war. To strike is to burn your own house down. It is not a good thing. You have to be ready to fight. I know you always have to be ready to fight, but every time we have had a strike, it has been awful. And there are guys who would disagree with me, but we had a strike, the company I was working for was collapsing, I had a huge mortgage, and I thought I was going to go bankrupt. I was so nervous I couldn't write. I remembered my own father having a nervous breakdown when he was in the same situation.

I got down on my knees, and I said to God, "All I really care about are my sons. They're all that matters. Maybe the best thing for them is not to grow up in a house with a swimming pool and German cars. Maybe they need to live in a little house like I lived in growing up." One time in my life I lived in a house with no indoor plumbing. My father said, "Rich people have a canopy over their beds, and we have a can o' pee under our beds." But I got on my knees, and I said, "If that's what's best for my sons, then let me do that. Let me embrace this. But if I go down, let me go down with my flag flying, not on my knees trying to write what I think the market wants to buy. Let me write what I want to see." I got up, and I started writing a story called "Love and Honor," which is the story that led me to *Braveheart*.

You've got to walk through the shadow of the valley of death. I don't know any other way. But it is the way to life. C. S. Lewis said, "If you write for the approval of critics or the applause of the audience, you have no hope of writing anything worth reading. But if you write to tell the truth as you know it and for the love of the craft, then what you write will be worth reading." I didn't mean to preach a sermon, but there you go.

The Inspiration for Stories

I'd like to be more secular, but what I read and what I'm trained in deals with the search for spiritual meaning. A theologian said, "The genius of Jesus is that he found the holy, not among the monastic, but among the profane." Another said, "Religion is man's way to God, and is always erroneous, and revelation is God's way to man, and is always perfect." I say that to say that I don't believe in my own dogma. I have loads of dogma. I grew up a Southern Baptist in tent revivals. We went to twenty hours of church a week some weeks. I wouldn't trade it for anything, but I am full of dogma. I love it, I discuss it all the time inside my own head, but I don't believe my understanding is what I'm trying to get at.

What I really want is for the audience to feel. My father was a salesman, and he said, "People will remember almost nothing of what you say and only very little more of what you do, but all their lives they'll remember the way you made them feel." All their lives. I remember going to movies when I was a child. I would go to a movie and come out and think, "My life will never be the same because of what I just saw." It's how it made me feel. A lot of times I couldn't articulate that feeling with words. It would almost be like a song.

I'll give y'all an example from *Secretariat*. *Secretariat* is a terrific movie. It is all heart and I wanted to use the hymn "Oh Happy Day." Now I'll tell you how I understood this. Martin Luther King Jr. stood up in front of the world and said, "The children of slaves and the children of slave owners will sit down together at the table of brotherhood." And somebody killed him. And Bobby Kennedy got killed. And students got killed at Kent State during the protests. And then there was a massacre at My Lai, and a bunch of American boys had killed a bunch of innocent civilians. And the world just looked awful. In that time, children of slaves, against all rationality, sang a song called "Oh Happy Day." And everybody—you didn't have to be Christian, you didn't even have to be American—could hear the joy in that song. And it was around that same time that this racehorse named Secretariat came along and ran. He was pure. He was incorruptible. And I saw those two events, which had no rational linkage . . . In the soul, they were linked. I've listened to "Oh Happy Day" my whole life. I felt this joy. And I wanted the movie to have that. There were a lot of people saying, "What does 'Oh Happy Day' have to do with the racehorse?" And my answer was, "Everything."

In one of the first test screenings I was sitting next to a friend from Disney—she was a casting director there—and I was worried about the music. The song came up at, "Jesus washed, he washed our sins away." It's unmistakable in the lyric, but I wasn't trying to convince people to be Christians. I don't think my own understanding is sufficient to convince people of my dogma, but I think if I love and I can get them to love what I love, then we've connected the circuit with God.

I wondered how my friend was going to take "Oh Happy Day." At the end of the movie, I look over, and tears are streaming down her face. She says, "I'm Jewish. I want them to sing 'Oh Happy Day' at my funeral." And I went into the men's room, and there was a gang member singing "Oh

Happy Day." And I went, "That's the right song." They felt what I wanted them to feel, from different perspectives. But that's what I'm looking for.

The executive who bought *Braveheart*, the one to whom I told the story, she's the daughter of Sydney Pollack, Rebecca Pollack. Sydney Pollack was one of the greatest directors who ever lived. His daughter Rebecca was a studio executive. I told her in ten minutes the story of William Wallace, and she went, "Go write that." I said, "You want an outline? You want a treatment?" She went, "What, you think I'll tell you how to write act two? Go write that." That kind of impulse . . . She believes in movie moments, that there are definitive moments when the audience's love meter just snaps and goes, "I'm with him. Whatever else happens, I'm with him." For me, in *Braveheart*, it's probably when the girl brings him—snaps off the thistle and gives him the flower—his father's grave—and he gives it back to her. I didn't know that was going to happen when I was writing it. That was not in an outline. That was not in any historical documents.

I thought, "If he goes back to this village, has he remembered anybody, and why?" And I felt, "Maybe he would have remembered one of the girls." I had them go out on a date. And here's this great warrior, and he can't talk to her. He doesn't know what to say to her. And they go out riding, and she goes, "Well, why didn't he . . .? If he wanted me to go riding with him, why doesn't he say something to me?" And they're about to part for the night. I'm writing this stuff, and I'm going, "Well, gosh, he needs to say something." I can feel her going, "Well, why doesn't he say something? He needs to say something." I didn't have anything I could think of for him to say, so she turns in disappointment to walk inside, thinking, "Well, he doesn't really like me." And he catches her hand. I didn't know he was going to catch her hand until I wrote it. He catches her hand, and I'm thinking, "Well, maybe he gives her something. Maybe he brought something to give her." And then he gives her back the thistle, and it was like, "I didn't know that was going to happen, but, man, I like this guy. I think women are going to like him too."

During the testing of the movie, one of the key players in the process walked into the editing room, and I was sitting in there with Mel Gibson, and this guy said, "Listen, all this stuff you guys are putting in the movie about women . . . Women aren't going to like this movie. This movie is for fourteen-year-old boys." And I went, "You're dead wrong!" And then we do the first test screening, and when they killed her, for the women in the

40   CONTINUED: 40

        Murron has grabbed a cloak off the back of the door; she runs
        out to hop up behind William, and they gallop away.

41   THE RIDE - AFTERNOON   41

        William and Murron race along the heather, up and down hills,
        through swollen streams. The rain stopped, as the sun sets;
        the Scottish mists lift, revealing stunning natural beauty.

42   William stops the horse and they look out over it all   42
        together. He speaks, without turning to face her.

                            WILLIAM
                Your father doesn't like me, does he?

                            MURRON
                It's not you. He dislikes that you're a
                Wallace. He just says... the Wallaces
                don't seem to live for very long.

                            WILLIAM
                Thank you for accepting.

                            MURRON
                Thank you for inviting.

                            WILLIAM
                I'll invite you again, but your mother
                thinks I'm crazy.

                            MURRON
                You are. And I'll come again.

        He lingers; he wants to say something, or maybe he just
        doesn't want the moment to end. Finally he spurs the horse.

43   EXT. THE MACCLANNOUGH HOUSE - NIGHT   43

        They reach the door. William hops off the horse and reaches
        up to help her down.

        The moment she touches the ground, they look into each
        other's eyes... but the door is snatched open so quickly by
        her mother that there is no time for a kiss.

                            MOTHER MacCLANNOUGH
                Murron, come in!

        He walks her closer to the door. They turn and look at each
        other again. She waits for him to kiss her...

                            MOTHER MacCLANNOUGH
                Murron, come in!

                                                          (CONTINUED)

43   CONTINUED: 43

          She still hesitates; he isn't going to kiss her. She starts
          in, but he grabs her hand. And into it he puts something he
          has taken from his pocket; it is wrapped in flannel. He hops
          on his horse, glances at her, and gallops away.

          She stands in the open doorway; she looks down at what he
          left her. She unwraps the flannel; it is a dried thistle,
          the one she gave him years before.

44   EXT. WALLACE FARM - DAY   44

          William is re-thatching the roof of his barn, when he hears
          riders approaching, and looks down to see that it is
          MacClannough, backed by Campbell and Hamish.

                              MACCLANNOUGH
                    Young Wallace--

                              WILLIAM
                    Sir, I know it was strange of me to
                    invite Murron to ride last night. I
                    assure you, I--

                              CAMPBELL
                    MacClannough's daughter is another
                    matter. We come to fetch you to a
                    meeting.

                              WILLIAM
                    What kind of meeting?

                              CAMPBELL
                    The secret kind.

          William goes back to repairing his roof.

                              CAMPBELL
                    Your father was a fighter. And a
                    patriot.

                              WILLIAM
                    I know who my father was. I came back
                    home to raise crops. And, God willing, a
                    family. If I can live in peace, I will.

          Campbell shakes his head and reins his horse away, with
          Hamish. MacClannough lingers.

                              MACCLANNOUGH
                    You say you wanna stay out of the
                    troubles. Prove to me you can, and you
                    may court my daughter. Until you prove
                    it, my answer's no.

                                                        (CONTINUED)

audience, there was not enough that we could do to the English that was sufficient. The women were the ones that wanted retribution.

And then in the final scene the axe is dropping toward William Wallace's throat. I can see myself sitting in the room of my house—the same room where I said that prayer, by the way. I was writing that the axe was falling toward his throat. And I knew we wanted to see the axe fall, but I knew we could not film the axe hitting his throat. That just wasn't ever going to be in the movie. So I thought, "Well, what do we show?" And, you know, this is really funny, I say I write from the point of view of each character, but ultimately I also write from the point of view of an audience member.

The axe is dropping toward William Wallace's throat. I wrote that, and I thought, "What happens in the last fraction of a second of his life?" And I thought, "Well, let's be with him. Let's be with him as the axe is falling and he knows it." What would he do? And I thought, "Maybe he would turn and look for his friends." And I wrote, "Then Wallace, at the last fraction of a second of his life, turned his eyes to find his friends, because he knew they would be there." Not until that moment did I know she was between them.

And I wept. I wrote it, and I wept. And I think that if you're not prepared to go to that place, then you should not be a writer. I think you should find another ambition. I think you should go find something that would prevent you from having to look for what would move you enough to make you weep in front of a group of strangers, because that's what you do when you make a movie. You want a group of people to open up their hearts and strip away the walls and the fears, because in a theater, we're naked. The screen in us, the screen in our hearts, it's the most powerful medium that anyone has ever created for communicating that. It has music. It has narrative. It has intimacy. It has grandeur. That, to me, is part of what I want to feel when I'm doing a movie. What's hard for me when I'm writing is when I don't want to feel that, when I am so angry, when I am so afraid, when I am so—whatever—in my own crap, that I don't want to go to that place and I just write crap. And it's like . . . A screenplay is a prayer.

I wrote it, and I wept. . . . If you're not prepared to go to that place, then you should not be a writer. . . . You should find another ambition.

245 CONTINUED: 245

We are spared seeing the cutting: we are ON WILLIAM'S FACE as
the disembowelment begins. The Magistrate leans in beside
him.

                    ROYAL MAGISTRATE
          It can all end. Right now! Bliss.
          Peace. Just say it. Cry out. "Mercy!"
          Yes? ...Yes?

The crowd can't hear the magistrate but they know the
procedure, and they goad William, chanting...

                    CROWD
          Mer-cy! Mer-cy! Mer-cy!

William's eyes roll to the magistrate, who signals QUIET!

                    ROYAL MAGISTRATE
              (booming)
          The prisoner wishes to say a word!

SILENCE. Hamish and Stephen weep, whisper, pray...

                    HAMISH/STEPHEN
          Mercy, William... Say Mercy...

William's eyes flutter, and clear. He fights through the
pain, struggles for one last deep breath, and screams...

                    WILLIAM
          FREEEEE-DOMMMMMM!

The shout RINGS through the town.

246 Hamish hears it.   246

247 The Princess hears it, at her open window, and touches her   247
     tummy, just showing the first signs of her pregnancy.

248 Longshanks and his son seem to hear; the cry STILL ECHOES as 248
     if the wind could carry it through the ends of Scotland;

249 and Robert the Bruce, on the walls of his castle, looks up   249
     sharply, as if he has heard...

250 IN THE LONDON SQUARE   250

     the crowd has never seen courage like this; even English
     strangers begin to weep. The angry, defeated Magistrate gives
     a signal. They cut the ropes, drag William over and put his
     head on the block. The executioner lifts his huge axe -- and
     William looks toward the crowd.

251   THE CROWD, WILLIAM'S POV   251

     He sees Hamish, eyes brimming, face glowing...

252   SLOW MOTION - THE AXE   252

     begins to drop.

253   WILLIAM'S POV   253

     In the last half-moment of his life, when he has already
     stepped into the world beyond this one, he glimpses

254   someone standing at Hamish's shoulder. She is beautiful,   254
     smiling, serene.

     She is Murron.

255   We do not see the blade strike; but we see WILLIAM'S HAND as 255
     it does, his fingers opening to release the handkerchief
     which floats delicately down

                                         DISSOLVE TO:

256   EXT. SCOTTISH HIGHLANDS - DAY   256

     Robert the Bruce, flanked by the noblemen and the banners of
     the Scottish throne, and backed by a ragtag army of Scots,
     sits on his horse and looks down at the English generals in
     their martial finery.

                        ROBERT (V.O.)
               After the beheading, William Wallace's
               body was torn to pieces. His head was
               set on London bridge, where passersby
               were invited to jeer at the man who had
               caused so much fear in England.
                  (beat)
               His arms and legs were sent to the four
               corners of Britain as a warning.
                  (beat)
               It did not have the effect that
               Longshanks planned.

257   The English are haughty, victorious, at the head of their   257
     colorful, polished army, awaiting the ceremony of submission
     from Scotland's new king.

                        ROBERT (V.O.)
               And I, Robert the Bruce, backed by a body
               of Scottish veterans, rode out to pay
               homage to the armies of the English King,
               and accept his endorsement of my crown.

I believe when you're writing and you feel you're getting out of your own way that is what is divine and deeper than all of us. We're all individuals, but we're all alive, and that life is God. God is in that life. And I think a big part of writing is listening to God.

I was about to say I'm a lot more mature now than I used to be, but I'm sure that's not true. The idea of compromise drives me crazy, that we're not doing it the absolute best way we know. But what I think has to go with that feeling is humility, in the sense that somebody else may have a better idea or a perspective that will bring us to another idea, and we can talk about it openly enough to find out why the person doesn't want to do it our way. That's one aspect of it. There's another aspect about screenwriting that's even deeper. I think when you're writing a screenplay you should write without any consideration for whether something is filmable or not. You do not let yourself—in your directing head—limit your writing. Write whatever you can imagine. Then when it comes to being filmed, the realities can actually be more inspiring.

I'll give another example from *Secretariat*. We had a really small budget for *Secretariat* relative to . . . I don't know how many of y'all saw *Seabiscuit*, but our budget for *Secretariat* was a third of *Seabiscuit*'s. And we had a scene with a character named Eddie Sweat. He was Secretariat's groomer, and his hands were on Secretariat more than any other human being. So, though he was not the legal owner, that was his horse. And there's a moment in the movie in which Secretariat, before the Kentucky Derby, has been ill. Now, there was a scene in the screenplay in which Eddie walks in and Secretariat eats. And that's really all that happened. That scene was sort of necessary, but I just didn't know how to make it interesting as a director.

We were about to tear down the set—the finish line of the Kentucky Derby—and the guy said, "Randall, we're going to tear down the set. You need to shoot anything else?" Then I went, "God, it's so beautiful." And then I had an idea, and I went, "Go get Eddie." Nelsan Ellis, great actor. I scribbled some stuff down on the back of a legal pad, and I handed it to him and said, "I want you to walk out on the track and shout this." And he walks out on the track, and he shouts these words: "Hey, Kentucky! Big Red ate his breakfast this morning! And you're about to see something like you ain't never seen before!" Every time that scene plays, the audience cheers. That's the movie moment, but it's a moment that came out of a complete . . . I would have looked at it as a compromise. I guess that's really my point, to always be open to possibility. They tell me in *Raiders of the Lost Ark*, when Indiana Jones shoots the guy with the big scimitar, that was unscripted. Or, actually, it got scripted in the moment. Harrison Ford's back was hurting, and he was supposed to do all sorts of other stuff, and he went, "My back hurts. Why don't I just shoot?" And then it became the great moment.

Writing for Love. And Career.

Write what you love, but you've got to survive, you've got to make a living, and you've got to be in dialogue with other people who may not love what you love or may want to do something that feels to you like it's in real contradiction to what you love. I don't want to make it seem as if I'm saying that it's always worked. In a way, I guess it has worked, but there have been many, many years when I've been in the middle of feeling that I'm writing what I love, and nobody's biting.

John Hancock tells a great story. You may have heard this. He went to California for the first time and got a meeting with Kevin Reynolds, this really successful director. And Kevin Reynolds said to him, "If I give you some advice, will you promise to take it?" And John said, "Yes. I will." And he said, "Go home. Either you will take my advice, or you will live in defiance of me and keep finding a way to go on." And I think that's what it is for me, the sense that God is shining on me. I don't think there's any doubt that I've got rewards and things that I feel like I didn't earn. But I also know it can be a really wretched place when you have money and even some notoriety and even some attention, and you still don't feel that you've done anything. And what works in both of those places, I think, is to keep trying to get what you love into the situation you're in.

I've learned a great deal in writing television and all sorts of other things, and I think we all have to ask ourselves all the time, "What do I do now?" I tell you, it's a really funny thing. The time after *Braveheart* won all of those Oscars was one of the worst periods of my whole life. My marriage fell apart, I felt isolated from all my friends . . . My only answer was to put one foot in front of the other, to put my pains and my worries and my anger all into the furnace and use that as energy to keep going. And what I did next was, I wrote a story about men who were . . . I was offered *The Man in the Iron Mask*, and on the surface it didn't have anything to do with what I was feeling, but on this deeper level I thought, "Okay, this is about guys in their forties who have achieved fame, and now the world treats them as if they're irrelevant." And that's the way I felt after *Braveheart*, like everybody would say, "Oh, you did *Braveheart*. Well, you can't do anything like that again." I thought, "Well, I will be me in this story. I'll keep trying to bring that struggle into my writing." Even to find a place in which . . . Again, I'm far too personal, but during *We Were Soldiers*, my father died, and my wife of twenty years and I divorced. I had a lot to deal with. It wasn't until this point that I felt I could make a movie about joy. So my sense is that that is our journey, and that every time you put a pen to paper, you're performing an act of courage and faith.

On Rewriting

I think it was T. S. Eliot that said, "I've had a great day writing. This morning I put in a comma, and this afternoon I took it out." And I don't think he was just being an Irishman when he said that. I think he was meaning that you get to a point at which you've considered everything, and you go, "You know, this is the best I can make it."

I want to be practical about this, as well as theoretical. I have a really great friend, Jack Bernstein—Jack wrote the original *Ace Ventura: Pet Detective*. Jack and I are really close. Jack is a liberal Jew from Miami. I am a conservative Baptist from Tennessee. We are the best of friends. I couldn't do without him. Jack is the guy I trust to give the roughest of my rough drafts, because I can hand him what I'd be embarrassed to show anybody else, and he'll find what's good in it. He understands what's bad in it, but he'll go, "Well, you know, this is intriguing to me." And that's the stage of, "I know it's good enough to give to Jack." And then it's like, "How do I know when it's good enough to give to somebody else?"

There's always, for me, a big, hold-your-breath . . . No matter how many times I've written, no matter how many screenplays I've written, no matter how many revisions I've written, I've had to take a deep breath to let the script go and let somebody read it. But I think there's still an internal mechanism to go, "I've taken this one as far as I can get it." I also think, by the way, sometimes I have to write and sometimes I have to put the screenplays aside for a while. In *Braveheart*, I wrote twelve drafts before I called it "draft one." There were twelve drafts. I'll set it aside for a little bit and go on and work on something else, and then I'll go back to it, read it again and study it. But I keep going through it top to bottom.

My writing approach is, "Just start and keep going." Give yourself a quota of pages. You have to. I have to. Maybe you write differently. Give yourself permission to write badly. Embrace that. Do it. Just keep the pencil moving or your fingers going. If I do five pages a day, it doesn't make any difference whether they're any good. The next day, I may go, "Oh, you know, I'm gonna change the story from what I had in those previous pages." I don't go back. I just write as if it were already changed. Just keep going. A character may be a woman on page 15, she may be a man on page 45. I'll figure that out later. Just keep going. Then I'll go back to page one and start again.

I'll go through, and the ending may be, she kills him, and then he kisses her, and they get married, and he shoots her, and they all live happily ever after. I mean, I may do that to give myself a rough, dead ending, but I don't know what the beginning is until I know what the ending is. So I keep going back and forth, like a woman with long hair, just combing. If I get a snag, I don't try to tear my way through it. I skip over it and work that snag out later. That's how I do it.

There's so much filmmaking consciousness now that didn't exist when I grew up, and it largely is a technical issue. Somebody—I think it was Paramount—recently made a deal or set up a little fund for people to make movies with their cell phone cameras. And now we have editing equipment, and you can, on your Mac, do all sorts of things. And by the way, in *Secretariat*, we have the most eye-popping horse-racing footage I have ever seen, and a lot of that was shot with an $800 camera. If we can do that, then the means of making a movie gets more and more accessible. But the need to tell a story that holds together in feature-film length is still the economical way to do pictures. All of it is, so far, sustainable in the entertainment medium.

I think there is the danger of becoming so practical-minded that you don't continue to reach. I was in my forties when I wrote *Braveheart*, so one of the things I tell my students at Pepperdine is, "You're sitting there feeling all this pressure that you don't know your greatest story or what your definitive story is yet." And a lot of those pressures, I felt. If I can't tell my parents why I want to do this writing thing instead of going to law school, and if I can't justify it for myself, I'll never have the chance to follow my dreams. And there is a horrible bit of pressure that goes with that. So everyone feels, "Well, I have to write the great screenplay before I'm nineteen," and I just have to say, "That didn't happen for me." Margaret Mitchell wrote one book, ever. Only one. Worked on it ten or twelve years. One book. *Gone with the Wind*. And I think if that were the only one most anybody wrote, most people would feel that was a pretty great career.

I think a great thing to do—I don't follow this principle, mind you—is to try to listen more than you talk. I think it's really important to be as good as you can be as a writer, but if we're only talking, only writing, and not living, then our writing is empty. Some people start making films when they're too young . . . It's one thing to have the perspective of youth, but don't just make films all the time. Do other things. I think writers ought to act. I think writers ought to play sports and exercise. I think they ought to do community service. I think they ought to build things. A lot of writers have been carpenters. William Faulkner worked in a post office. When he finally had a bestseller, he said, "No longer do I have to be at the beck and call of every SOB who has two cents to buy a postage stamp." But it was probably good for him to do those other jobs, too.

If I have a message it would be, "Try to take the pressure off yourself." And I think the way you do that is by writing every day. You can find an hour or two to write every day, but you can't write eight hours a day. I can't write eight hours a day. Write some every day and do some other things, and those other things will help sustain you and take the pressure off. But if you're here, and you're not writing five days a week, then you're not going to be happy. That's why you're here, I think.

When to Stop Researching and Start Writing

Do not research. Research is a bad thing. I mean it. If you know enough about the story to be interested in writing a screenplay, write the screenplay. Then, when questions come up, go back and look those up specifically. It's just fact-checking then. Research is not what people go to the movies to see; it's the why of the story. The heart of the story is the how, but the soul of the story is the why. Just write with your heart. You know about something, and whatever it is about that thing that made it rattle around in your head, your knowledge of it is superior to 99% of any people who are going to see the result of your labors just by the simple fact that you're interested in it. It's like, "Well, I'm interested in this story because there's a moment in here when I know this woman went out on the front porch with a shotgun. I'm interested in that moment." Write that story.

When I heard about William Wallace, I knew, standing there at the gates of Edinburgh Castle, that there would be a scene in that story where he's standing in front of the men on the battlefield, and they're outnumbered. So I wrote that scene. It was later when I found out, "Okay, William Wallace was a general, and he won the Battle of Stirling Bridge. Oh, okay, then I'll call it 'The Battle of Stirling Bridge.'" What I was most interested in was, what would he say on that battlefield to make someone stay? What would make me stay if I were one of those warriors?

We shot it in Ireland, and there were all these guys . . . We used the Irish Army Reserve. We didn't even have to give them haircuts. They showed up looking like they were . . . And the first scene I ever saw filmed of any of my work was the speech at the Battle of Stirling Bridge. I just arrived in Ireland, and I'm waiting for this scene to shoot, and there's seven cameras going, and all of these hours being dressed up as Scottish warriors, and their axes are rubber, and their spears are over their heads hitting each other, and they're Irishmen. They're all painted up in blue, and they're waiting for this to go, and the seven cameras are all set up, and then they call, "Action!" Mel Gibson comes riding out on his horse, and the horse can smell his adrenaline. The horse is just jerking every which way, and it's perfect for the scene. His head's kind of bobbing this way and back, and the wind's whipping his hair across his face, and you know, "Sons of Scotland, I am William Wallace!" And all 3,000 of these Irishmen are just like, "Argh!"

He goes, "And I see before me a whole army of my countrymen coming in defiance of tyranny," and the electricity is going through our spines. And he goes, "You've come to fight as free men, and free men you are. But what will you do with your freedom? Will you fight?" And what is supposed to happen is, one of the guys is supposed to step forward and go, "No, not against that. We'll run, and we'll live." And then he finishes the speech about, "Yeah, you'll run, and you'll live, at least for a while," you know, and the whole dying-in-your-bed thing, but these are Irishmen. And there are 3,000 of them, and they're dressed in battle war paint. He goes, "You've come to fight as free men, and free men you are. But what will you do with your freedom? Will you fight?" And all 3,000 of these Irishmen go, "Yeah!" so seven cameras: "Cut!" "Cut!" "Cut!" "Cut!" "Cut!" "Cut!" "Cut!" Then Mel says, "Look, guys, this is a movie. We're not going to kill anybody today." And what was really funny, the previous day, they had been the Englishmen. But if there had been any Englishmen on the other side of the field, they would have killed them, because the moment was real. That does not come from research. It comes from the living moment.

My point is, I always thought—and I've tried this through trial and error—if you say to yourself, "If I don't know enough about the subject to write about it yet, then I will read two books," your sense of your own ignorance grows faster than your confidence in reading. You go, "Well, I have read these books, but I know that there are these other things that I need to read too. Now I need to read five." And it recedes from the impulse of why you wanted to write in the first place.

I wanted to write the story for that moment. I wanted to get to, "You may take my life, but you will never take my freedom." I wanted to hear that guy stand up and say that. To me, the life of writing is the life of nurturing your own enthusiasm, your own passion for writing. You've got to nurture it. If you don't like it, change it until you do like it. I'll finish a first draft—a rough draft—and I'll turn it over, and I'll pen it out, and I'll turn it over, and I'll write, "This sucks, because . . ." And with my friend Bernstein, I'll ask him, "What do you hate about it?"

"Well, you know, there's none of 'this' in it. There's not enough of 'that' in it. I mean, what would it be like if you liked it?"

"Well, it would have the same . . . Blah, blah, blah." And it's asking those kinds of questions. But you've got to be in love with it. And I don't mean that you don't do research, but sometimes, at the very minimum, write your pages while you're doing the research. The other problem about research is that we find out something, and because it's taken us a long time to find it out, we want it in our story. Then it's really hard to go, "Well, I know they used to call . . . In the 1880s, the Democrats called the Republicans 'copperheads,' so I'm going to put that in there," or something. What makes the story have bite is that it feels relevant to people.

What makes the story have bite is that it feels relevant to people.

2

Story

The process of finding the story you have to tell is wondrous, frustrating, humiliating, and joyous. It is an all-encompassing experience. ★ PETER HEDGES (*About a Boy, What's Eating Gilbert Grape*)

What Makes a Great Story

A Conversation with Bill Wittliff

I'm very different from a lot of writers in that I never want to know in advance what's going to happen. If I know what I'm going to write before I write, there's no sense of discovery left for me. There's no journey, no adventure. Usually what I do when I write an original, I start with either a character that interests me or an event. If I start with a character, then I bump the character against an event to see how the character responds. Even one event will slightly change that character. Then you bump that new character against another event and he will react differently than he would have before the first event changed him. If your character comes alive, you start following him. For me that's the great joy of writing. It's when, as a writer, I totally disappear and become both an observer and a participant. But I never want to know what's going to happen in advance. I don't think it's a particularly smart way to write because when you get in a jam, you don't really know how you got there because you didn't think your way there, you felt your way in . . .

What Makes a Great Character

For me, the best stories are about characters that you genuinely care about in a story that really moves you. If you have a moving story but not a moving character then you're just telling a story. But if you have that combination, a moving character in a moving story, then you have a chance to find meaning both in the character and in what the story can deliver in terms of that character. I know that sounds a little awkward. Basically, drama is complicated, but at its base it's very simple. Drama is conflict. I want to get through that door, and some guy says, "I'm not going to let you through that door." Now you have conflict. Then the story becomes, how does this character get through this door, and some guy isn't going to let him. That creates drama.

I get a lot of young people who want to talk about drama and story, and I tell them if you're writing a story where this happens, and then this happens, and then this happens, and then this happens, that's not an interesting story. There's not a dynamic there. An interesting story is, this happens, and then this happens, but then *this* happens. A perfect example of this is *Jaws*. It starts with a girl calmly swimming out to the bell. Then something hits her from underneath. You've just created a dynamic. What happened? She's disappeared, and you haven't seen the monster. You're creating it in your head. Spielberg was brilliant at that with *Jaws* because it's a long time before you see the shark. You see the effect of the shark, so it's working in the mind.

The trick to telling a story is not to tell everything. It's to tell just enough so the audience is leaning forward, waiting to see what's going to happen next. Meanwhile you give them enough so that they can anticipate what might happen next. If you give them signals to anticipate and you don't deliver, you better one-up it or they will be disappointed. Screenwriting is much more like writing poetry—the real juice is not in the lines but that space between the lines. If the lines are done right, the audience makes the jumps. If you tell them everything, they're just observers. If you do it right, they're participants. That's what you want. That's what all great art does. It makes the audience a participant instead of just an observer.

Developing Voices for Your Characters

I've got a pretty good ear, and I listen to people. I always have. I come from a country family, all of whom were great storytellers and great at mimicking other country folk. It just kind of comes natural in my bloodline. The trick is just carefully listening to people. There are certain rhythms of speech depending on what part of the country you're in. It used to be what county you're in. Dialogue is revelatory of character. Also, the silences, the space between words. You just listen. When the characters take over, they tell you how they want to talk, and they tell you what they want to say.

Building Tension

You build tension by letting the audience in on a piece of information that the characters in the film don't have. Hitchcock said it best—what you do, you show a lovely couple, and you love the couple because they're so sweet. Then you send them out to dinner. And while they're out, a guy crawls under the house and loads up fifteen sticks of dynamite under the living room floor and sets a clock. So we know there's a bomb that's going to explode. Then he switches to the young couple eating dinner, and then coming home. And you cut between them and that ticking clock. That's tension. Is it going to blow up before they get there? That's tension. Number one, it's about caring about the characters; number two, letting the audience in on something that's going to affect those characters unless they get out of harm's way. There are other ways to create tension—the desire of characters, a story about someone who is desperate to attain a certain thing. You can create a lot of tension by showing how close they come to their goal without reaching it or the hurdles they have to jump.

The tension in *Black Stallion* initially was on the ship when the horse was locked up in the corral on the boat. The ship was burning and was about to go down, and nobody was concerned about that horse except the kid. The fire's raging, the boat's sinking, the poor horse is locked up, the kid releases the horse, and it jumps over the side. And the next thing that happens is the same kind of thing—the horse is in the water, but it's tangled in all these ropes, and you think it's going to drown. It regains its balance. Meanwhile the kid is about to drown, but when the horse swims by, the kid is able to grab the rope, and it is the horse that pulls him to the shore. Another one in *The Black Stallion* is when the kid wakes up and there is a snake. The snake coils and hisses and is just about to strike, and the black stallion stomps the snake and kills it. What's important here, always, is that you care about that kid and you care about that horse. Otherwise you're telling a story with no emotion.

Whatever story the storyteller wants to tell, he or she tells it from or through a certain place with people that are believable as people in that place. Or you can go the other way and bring outsiders in. The place is as important to cast as your lead actors, in my view.

Lonesome Dove, the novel, is about this group of ex–Texas Rangers down on the Rio Grande River. Lonesome Dove is just this tiny little town, but that town was as much a character in that miniseries as the actors. What we did, we went down to the Rio Grande, and we found a spot that was both harsh and barren but visually interesting because you could see the Rio Grande from both directions. We simply built Lonesome Dove, and nowhere did it have a sign that said Lonesome Dove. Everybody who was there knew it was Lonesome Dove. That's how careful you try to be with this stuff. It all has a logic.

The other thing about place—and this is important if people want to get into film—is actors. Their performances will be much better if you put them in a setting authentic to the story you're trying to tell. That's true of costume, too. They absolutely feed off a place, feed off what they're wearing and how they look. It helps them transform whoever they are in real life into whoever they are in the film, which can sometimes be an even more real life, which is great film. That's what happened on *Lonesome Dove*. Tommy Lee and Duvall . . . I was with both those guys when they got their costumes. When Robert Duvall put that hat on and sucked his teeth and smoothed his mustache, he was transformed. He became Gus at that moment. It was awesome.

I saw that happen with Sissy Spacek too. She put on a housedress for a little film I had written called *Raggedy Man*. She looked at herself in the mirror, and all of a sudden, she became Nita. What's important is that those costumes be right, the settings and the furniture be right, because it makes them believe they are in this other world, and then they become an integral part of it.

Things are important like Gus's hat, or if he wore a certain kind of boot, or if he had a pocket watch that belonged to his father. I will write minutia like that into the script knowing that sometimes it will be ignored, but also knowing that a sensitive actor will get it and will demand that watch because it gives him or her a little piece of business that they can relate to when they do the scenes. You can also do that with physical gestures. I didn't write Gus sucking his teeth and doing that thing with his mustache. That was a piece of business that Duvall came up with that absolutely made that character more real and more individual. You'd never seen that before in any character or any film, and that was Duvall's. As a writer, anything like that that illuminates the character, I'll write it in absolutely.

Common Mistakes to Avoid

I would guess that the most common mistake new writers make is that they are hesitant to accept the responsibility of creating new worlds. Unless you're doing a nonfiction thing, you're casting yourself in a some-times-uncomfortable role as a little god. You're creating a world that, as of yet, does not exist in the real world. But if it's done right, like in great movies, those worlds become more real than the world we walk through and drive through everyday. Most young writers don't yet have the courage to accept that responsibility. I would urge young writers, the first time they write, don't reach too close, reach way out there. You may miss, but you may hit some things that you never would have dreamed you'd hit if you never reached for it.

So much of showbiz these days is about fame and riches. A lot of writers would like to have a piece of that. A lot of times they make the mistake of writing what they think the market might be interested in, rather than reaching deep down into their hearts and saying, "Here's something that matters to me. Here's something I genuinely want to say," and then being bold enough to say it.

Most film schools teach filmmaking and screenwriting through movies that have already been made. A lot of kids think they need to make *Star Wars*, *Citizen Kane*, whatever. Not a lot of film schools that I know teach them to reach down with both hands into their own beings to see what they have as unique individuals on this spinning globe. That's where the great storytellers come from: those that reach down to see what they have. You may miss, but you'll never know unless you reach.

The Tools That You Bring

I made a deal with myself some years ago that no one would see my first drafts, because if I thought people were going to see my first drafts, it would limit what I wrote. What's deepest in all our hearts as storytellers is this soul-deep desire to communicate. You want applause, you want people to approve. Sometimes you don't give yourself a chance to be really bad. I made the deal with myself. That way I could be as bad as it was possible to be, and I wasn't at risk. What I learned was about 70% of my first drafts were awful, but there was 30% that was better stuff than I ever would've gotten on paper if I was limiting myself because of fear of what people might think. I'd urge young writers, first write for the content of your heart. Don't worry about what other people might think. Just cut loose, let whatever inner urge they have to be writers, storytellers . . . Find a way to get it on the paper. Incidentally, I think writers write. And when it's good, they're glad and they keep writing, and when it's bad, they throw it away and they keep writing. I don't think there are any tricks or shortcuts to being a writer and writing well. Writers write. They write and rewrite and rewrite. At some point you either know it's as good as it can possibly be at that particular moment in your life, or you know you're just not mature enough yet to tell that story. So you just stay at it.

> I'm amused when some people say writing is so lonely. It's not. When the characters hit the paper and they're real flesh and blood and they're breathing and they're talking to you and they're talking through you, it's not lonely at all. You're sitting there with a roomful of people you've come to love and partially understand and who are doing interesting things. It's not lonely. It's the great joy of creation. It's great fun.

Recommended Reading

There are two books that I think are really terrific. One is by Stephen King and is called *On Writing*. It is a terrific book. Also, *The Courage to Create*, which is not just about writing but also about the courage to create. It's not about trying to get away from fear but using fear.

I've never read all the books on how to write a screenplay because I didn't want my stuff to become too mechanical. I feared that would happen if I knew too much about the craft. The guy who knows the most about writing screenplays is Shakespeare. If you read his comedies and his dramas not as literature but as how-to books, I'm telling you, he knew it all. He knew everything you need to know in terms of the craft. It's all there. As an American writer I'm probably more affected by Mark Twain. He had the heart and soul of all of us as Americans right at the tip of his pen. And not just for his generation. *Huck Finn* and *Tom Sawyer* are still as relevant today as they were when he wrote them. Of the more modern writers, the one that I'm most in awe of is Cormac McCarthy.

When I first started writing screenplays, I'd never seen a screenplay and knew nothing about it. I started going to movies and watching the movies for what had been written to create that movie. I would go two times. The first time, I'd just watch the movie. The second time, I would shift in my seat and watch the audience. Watching the audience taught me more than anything. You can tell everything by body language. You can tell when that film has them—they're sitting forward, they're not talking, they're hardly breathing. But when that story lets them go, they're slouching, looking around, coughing, whispering. If that story lets them go for 30 seconds, it'll take two to three minutes to get them back.

> If that story lets them go for 30 seconds, it'll take two to three minutes to get them back.

What young people should do if they're interested in film, they should look at every film they can get their eyes on, but not just good films. Look at bad films. "Why didn't this turkey work?" Usually you can see. Generally, the writer or director didn't have a point of view and confused the audience. Certainly, I would recommend reading voraciously—every subject, non-fiction, fiction, short stories. Films are more like poetry and short stories than novels. There are movies that I wouldn't say that about, like the second *Godfather*, which is just a work of genius.

> It's about instinct. It's not about intellectually designing something. If you start to become too conscious, I think it can inhibit you. You start thinking there's this model, and you have to have all these pieces. It's just a very odd process. What I was told was to read some great scripts and then sit down and write one. You learn to write by writing. ★ SACHA GERVASI (director of *Hitchcock*, writer of *The Terminal*)

More important than all that, really pay attention every moment to the world you're moving through as a person. Listen to the way your friends talk. Listen to what is hurting them, what their hearts say. Be a participant in your own life. And as a filmmaker maybe you can reveal some aspect of it to those of your generation who don't have the bent to do that. I think that's a great gift of writers, writers in whatever form. It's a high calling. If we do it right, we put models out into the world. We say, "This is a way you might consider living. This is a way you might not want to go. That way lies doom." People pay attention. They pay attention because writers are tricksters. We tell a lot of fibs to get at a truth. We're not preaching at them, we're telling a story. The underlying lesson of any good story is, "This is a way to live; this is a way not to live." That's a high calling and a great responsibility.

Steven Zaillian on Where the Story Originates

For me, the story usually originates with the world and a character. I need both. With *Bobby Fischer*, I wasn't interested in the chess world before, but when I started reading about it, it was kind of like a secret society. It was something I didn't know anything about. I was learning about it, and it was something that could be shown and something that could be explored. That's basically what the book was. It was a description, a series of articles that described the chess world. The Josh character did figure into some of those chapters, but not all of them. So I needed both. I needed the character and the world. For me, that's really important.

People always say to write about what you know. I usually write about stuff I don't know, because I like the process of learning about it. When Europeans come here, they'll come to Austin, and they'll take pictures. The pictures they take are going to be different from the pictures people from Austin take. They're going to see it in a different way. I want to discover something. *Awakenings* was about medicine, and I didn't know anything about medicine. The chess world, gangsters in the 1970s in New York, I didn't know anything about those things. The process of discovering is fun for me.

Peter Hedges on
Crafting Story

I think of a story like a great friendship: you meet somebody, you think you know them, you don't really know them, you've gone through a lot of battles with them and a lot of life, you've metaphorically made love—if it's that kind of movie—and there's been a death. You've been through a lot. You come to understand it. It's in your bones.

There are two types of stories for me. There's the "can't wait to tell" story, which is what *Dan in Real Life* was for me. I'm more of the school of "have to tell," which *Pieces of April* was and *Gilbert Grape* was. I couldn't wait to tell it, but there was a point where it tipped over to "I have to tell it." Only you can know what that story is that you can write.

The projects where I've had the most success are the ones where I thought, "I just want to write a story." *Gilbert Grape* was a story that my brothers might read, and that my grandmother could understand, a story that was easy to understand but hard to handle. I wanted it to be accessible. Instead of trying to figure out what they want and what they're going to buy, you should devote more of your time to the story that you might not fully understand yet. The story that you can comprehend quickly is probably not as interesting as the story that's going to unfold over a long period of time.

Lawrence Kasdan on
Story and Theme

When I started out, there would be ideas that I wanted to write about, and then I'd find a vessel to put them in. Sometimes they were genre vessels, and sometimes they were more free form. As time goes by, I've become less interested . . . There's a fabulous quote that I can't give you, but I think it's Yeats. He says the only thing that has a chance of being wonderful is something that doesn't try to teach, doesn't tell, doesn't demonstrate. It took me until today, I think, to understand that. I rigorously avoid thinking about theme now because your life has its themes, and if you do singular work, if you do auteur work, you are going to come through. Your themes are going to come through perfectly clear without you ever explicitly saying anything.

I was talking to Alvin Sargent, who is a great, great screenwriter. We were talking about how we always get stuck. We want the screenplay to be about narrative, because that's what American movies are about—narrative and story. But invariably our movies start with character. It's a curse. It's a terrible curse. But it's really the only way I can get started. I have a character I want to write about and that character bumps up against another character, and things start to happen. Alvin said to me, "It's horrible being like this. It's horrible not being a story person. When I die, I just want my tombstone to say, 'Finally a plot.'"

3

Process

I think everything has gotten harder. When you start out, you have a lot of energy to apply to these things, and things work, and you're very prolific. As you go on, it can slow down, and you feel like, "Oh, I've done this," or, "I've used that idea already," and you start editing yourself in a way that's not particularly useful. You say, "Oh, wow, this is just like a scene I wrote five years ago," and then you stop. You will take any excuse you have for stopping because stopping is a natural state of writing. ★ LAWRENCE KASDAN (*Body Heat, Raiders of the Lost Ark*)

A Conversation with
John Lee Hancock

A Perfect World

I wanted my script to be something that people read. I knew I'd probably never get paid, but I wanted it to be read. The first script that gets noticed is usually not made, but it hopefully gets you in the door. This one actually got me in the door and got made, which was the exception to the rule. That movie was called *A Perfect World*. I had never been to film school or anything, and so Clint Eastwood became my film school. He allowed me to be on the set, and to my knowledge, it's the first time he had done that. Not that he was against writers being on set, he's just very pragmatic and didn't see any use in it—"Why bring a writer out? I'm just going to shoot the movie, and he's not going to have anything to do." But I somehow convinced him that I wouldn't be in the way, and I wouldn't obstruct anything, and that I had a lot to learn, and I wanted to learn, and I wouldn't ask too many questions.

When I got there, Kevin Costner, who I had met when we worked on the script a little together, told me, "You write like a director."

I thought, "Gosh, that's a funny thing to say. I'm not sure if that's a compliment."

He said, "When I read your scripts, I see the visual imagery." He wasn't talking about "angle on" or "extra close-up" or anything like that. He was just talking about the imagery, what it evoked, and how provocative it was.

I said, "Well, that's great."

He goes, "Why don't you direct this movie?"

I said, "You've already got a director. His name's Clint Eastwood. He just won an Oscar for *Unforgiven*." Then I said, "And you won the one before that for *Dances with Wolves*."

Then he said, "You should prepare to direct this movie. You prepare every day with a shot list. You know the work. You've got the call sheet."

So I thought, "Wow, that's kind of a good exercise." And I did it. Every morning, I would come in while he was in makeup, and we would go through my shot list, and we'd go through it bit by bit. It was fantastic because I had to think about the day's work and prepare based on what I'd written on the page. And then I'd see it shot, talk to Kevin about it, get his two cents—and he always had very strong opinions—and then watch it. Sometimes you'd look at it and say, "Gosh, I think my way was better." Sometimes you'd imagine, "That's kind of what I had in mind." But the kicker to that was I was able to watch dailies, and I would see what Clint had shot, so it was an amazing film school for me.

We shot it in Austin and all around, and it was kind of a magical time. The movie came out, and thankfully I've been working nonstop ever since. It's going on twenty years now, which makes me somewhat of a dinosaur in Hollywood, so I'm hoping they don't kick me out soon.

Breaking In

As an independent contractor, it's always the next gig, the next gig, the next gig. I'm a house painter. Hopefully I paint someone's house, and the neighbor looks at it and says, "Who painted your house?"

If the owner says, "That Hancock guy! He does a good job." Boom. That's how it works.

It's a small town. It's a company town. It's a hard one to break into. There's no doubt about it. I think writing is the fastest track if you want to be in the creative side of it, if you want to write, or create, or direct, or all those kinds of things, because a script can open doors. You can have a script in hand. The way it was described to me by Kevin Reynolds, who is from Texas as well and a really talented filmmaker, "Remember when you were a kid? Did you ever move?"

I said, "Yeah, we moved once."

He said, "When you move to a new town, you try to make friends. You're a little boy, and you walk outside, and your mom says, 'Go play with the neighbor kids,' and you get out to the vacant lot, and you look, and they're playing football. You stay on the sidelines, watching, hoping that one of them will say, 'Hey, come on and play with us!' but they don't ever say that. Finally, you get enough confidence to say, 'Can I play?' and they kind of ignore you. Then it's your birthday, and your dad gives you a brand new football for your present. You take the football in arm and go down to the vacant lot. They see you with a new football, and they say, 'Hey, throw me the ball, kid!' and you start to throw it, you hesitate, and you go, 'I get to play.' That's what a script is. That football."

When you get that kind of notice, doors open unbelievably quickly for a script that people respond to. It's not a magic potion. There are still many steps to getting your movie made. It's next to impossible. It's a minor miracle when a movie is made. Congratulations to anyone who achieves that task. It almost has fairy dust sprinkled on it if it is successful, because, yes, it is an artistic endeavor, but it is such a community artistic endeavor. You have so many people working so hard on the movie. And sometimes the people that are trying the hardest to help make your movie great are the ones ruining it for you every day. It's a conspiracy. When you're directing a movie, everybody is there to foul up your movie every day, usually with the best of intentions. You have to keep on guard for that.

The doors opened for me with a script I didn't think would be marketable. I couldn't, for the life of me, figure out what the market was going to be. I could no more predict that than what prêt-à-porter in France is going to be in next year's fashion. I'm always going to be a little behind and just kind of . . . I'm not saying anyone should be stupid about the expectations of what's out there. You may say you have to write a certain movie, and I may say, "There's no market out there for that. That's gonna be next to impossible unless you completely do it yourself, and then it's gonna be hard to market."

I think it is important to write what moves you, and there's a way to tell . . . There's a great movie in every story. Somebody will come up and pitch you something, and you'll go, "You know, I don't see it, but that could be fantastic." Half the stuff I write, if I were to tell you in a line or two what it is, you'd go, "Doesn't sound interesting."

On Mentors

I went to Baylor. Kevin Reynolds's dad, Herb Reynolds, was the president of Baylor. Kevin had a baby sister named Rhonda Reynolds, who was closer to my age. Kevin was older. Kevin had gone to Baylor Law School, and he had come down to UT and taken film classes and went on to USC. He was a star there at the film program and had his first movie, *Fandango*, made there.

It's a terrific movie that really exposed Kevin Costner to the world, not so much that it did great business or anything, but people went, "Who's that guy?"

I was writing scripts in Houston, and I went, "Wait a minute. I went to Baylor. I went to Baylor Law School. I'm writing scripts. I've got a mentor. He just doesn't know it yet." So I set about to let him know I existed. Rhonda, unfortunately for Kevin, gave me his number, and I called and left a message with his agent at William Morris. I had a script, my first completed script. I didn't think at the time that it was very autobiographical, which is a tendency writers have with their first scripts. You write about something, and you go, "That's not me," but it's always you. They're never very good, unless your life is really fascinating.

Anyway, I decided I was going to move. I gave six months' notice to the law firm so I could clear my desk and moved to Los Angeles. I slept on my brother's couch. He was an engineer at Mobil and was going to be there for a very short time before moving back to Dallas. So I slept there and set about getting Kevin Reynolds to understand that he was my mentor. I kept calling and bugging him. I never got a call back. I sent the script to his agent and to his house thinking, "Here's my script. Once he reads this he's going to understand what a talent I am. He's going to want to mentor me."

Eventually, after bugging him . . . I don't think I was that much of a pest, but I would call him once a month. After six months or so, he calls one morning and says, "This is Kevin Reynolds. Is this John?"

"Yes, it's John."

"Can I buy you lunch?"

"Sure."

"Okay, Art's Deli, Studio City, one o'clock, Friday. That okay?"

"Uh, sure."

"Okay, see you there." There was no "Hi, how are you doing?" or anything like that.

I thought, "Well, he's a busy man. He recognizes my talent. We're going to have lunch, and it's all good. This is the way business is done. I get it now."

I get to Art's Deli. He's nice enough, and we're chatting about this and that and the other, and he says, "How can I help you?"

I said, "Well, I want to write. I want to direct movies. Did you get my script?" He said he had gotten it, so I said, "So what do you think? Did you read it?"

He said, "I read about ten pages. That's all I needed to read. I can tell that you're not without talent, and you need to write a whole lot more. Your dialogue's pretty good, but the scenes are misshapen. It's not the first pages of a movie that'll ever get made, but you're not without talent. I don't know what you're going to do if you don't write, but you should do that."

I thought, "Wow, this really isn't going like I thought it was going to. He's not recognizing me." So anyway, I finished my soup, and he's ready to go, and I explained, "I was kind of hoping for a mentor."

He said, "You get a mentor when you have something to bring to the table. If I have something to gain from mentoring you, that's when I'll be a mentor. Somebody may read a script for you or whatever, but all of us are shaking in our boots for our next job. It's not like a law firm, where you get old and gray, and they put you in a corner office, and you still get a piece of the profit. It's not that gig. The older you get, the more they are trying like hell to shove you out the door, because you don't represent what sixteen-year-old boys want to see in the theater."

So I said, "Okay, the mentor thing's out. What do I have left? I got him for lunch. It's probably going to take six more months to get another lunch with him, so I said, "I guess I would like your advice."

He said, "Will you take it if I give it?" and I said I would. So he said, "Go back to Houston and practice law." I was stunned. This really was not going well for me. He said, "If you take my advice, then you're not a writer. Just because some schmo tells you that you can't do it, if that's enough to send you back, you're not a writer. If you're pissed at me, and you leave here, and you go back home, and you write ten pages just to show me, then fine, my work is done. You're either a writer or you're not. You're either going to put in the work or not. I can't help you. Maybe you'll make it. Maybe you won't."

I fully expected when *A Perfect World* came out—because he and Costner were buddies—and I ran into him again, he would say, "You made it. Congratulations!" Instead, he was like, "Hey, good on you." That was it.

It was still the best advice I ever got in Hollywood, because if that's the advice you're going to take, you're never going to make it. During that time in Los Angeles there were lots and lots of talented, struggling writers. I look at the people who have succeeded and the people who haven't, and one of the pitfalls was that the people who didn't succeed ended up spending a lot of time bemoaning the fact that, "Oh, they're making *this* movie. This is crap. They cast him? Are you kidding me? This town is crap." That kind of pity party is what I hate.

The ones who were successful were overjoyed in determining their own future, declaring themselves, and defining their craft. They said, "I don't know about the market. I'm just really excited about writing this script," or, "I'm an actor, and I love being an actor. This is what I have to do." Those are the ones that have been successful. And that's kind of a good lesson. It'd be horrible if I said that the ones who succeeded were all the ones who thought only about the business and how to market themselves and those kinds of things. All of those things are important. Having a game plan is important, but not nearly as important as the fire in your soul. If you're a writer, you'll write. That's just it. It's always hard, but it's occasionally gratifying, and you live for the moments where it is.

The Beauty of Youth

It's in our DNA, or the genetic code or something, that we're filled with angst when we're in our late teens or twenties. That's how you're supposed to be. The world is hard, and you're fighting, and no one understands, and that's the beauty of youth. The older you get, you lose some of that, and maybe you give in a bit, and you have a little more wisdom or a different kind of wisdom. I think that's why societies work, because there's a mixture of young and old and all of these different ideas.

I didn't think my first script was autobiographical, but you tell me. It was about a young lawyer in Houston, Texas, and what he wanted to create with his life. How pathetic is that? I'm not saying there's not a movie there. It just wasn't one I could write. I'm trying to remember what my second script was. It was better.

People say to me all the time, "Well, you can get movies made now." And to a degree, I can, but even with the success of something like *The Blind Side*, I do adult drama. That's dead in Hollywood. It's really, really hard. I'm not saying not to do it. It's never dead forever, you know. Nobody's making Westerns, and then Clint gets to make *Unforgiven*. No one's doing adult drama, and then *The Town* does well. I'm always pulling hard for these movies because they mean I might have a job in the future, which is kind of important to my kids and me.

My first agent told me that it usually takes five scripts before you really make the medium work for you. I remember the first one, battling the medium a bit, because I was writing short fiction and plays, and saying, "How do I make this look on the page?" and "Now this looks right." You get to a place where format comes naturally. I think it's akin to someone learning to play chords on the guitar. Eventually you can play a song. Are you ready for Carnegie Hall? Probably not. It's how you pull the strings. And I think that just takes time and work. I think you feel yourself getting better and more adept, and then you find the medium working for you instead of battling it.

It took me a long time. There are some people that get it right out of the gate. God bless them. I'm not that talented. I had to work at it really, really hard. I think that I had a certain gift for dialogue, and I understood the rhythms and musicality of people's voices, as well as the energy of the scene and how it moves. I think that ended up being a strength I kept gravitating toward.

Struggling with Elements of the Craft

In the Blink of an Eye, by Walter Murch, is one of the best film books ever and talks about the experience of watching a movie, how we blink, and how we have internal cuts in our head when we watch something happening. We're constantly blinking, and cutting, and choosing to focus here or there. We experience films at 24 frames per second, which is probably not exactly how we blink, but it somehow seems the most real to us, when it's really just flickering still images in front of a light bulb cast on a wall or a screen or a sheet.

I think that when you read a script, it's a template for a movie. It's a blueprint. It's an artistic product too. Don't get me wrong. At the same time, you should try as much as you're able to make the experience of reading the script like watching a movie. I think it's very important. I've gotten much better at presenting on a page something to keep the reader's eyes dancing on the page, and then settling in, and then dancing. It's that kind of interplay that you're looking for. When it comes to action sequences especially, it's just trying to make the page as spare as possible, to set up the surprises, and things like that. And that's the thing I've hated. It's like, "Here we go. I've got to do this. I'll just buckle down and do it, and then revise, revise, revise, revise." But, you know, I still have difficulty with that.

How Do You Know When It's Good?

I'll go through the ups and downs of, "This is really good," to "Wow, this is bad." There's always one more problem. There's always one more thing. I've gotten much better at finishing first drafts that are closer to being ready because I've written so many, but it takes me longer to do a first draft than it used to because I know all the pitfalls and culs-de-sac I've been down before. I'll have a great idea and go, "I know where that's heading. In a week I'm going to toss this." You understand what's happening under the hood a lot more, but it makes you more cautious about doing things. You're throwing out about nine good ideas because, ultimately, you know they probably won't work.

It takes me longer to do an efficient draft. I'm usually pretty pleased to have finished, and then I'll do the thing where I'll go, "What's missing?" It's almost always a question that I can't answer before I start writing it because I find out through writing it what it's really about and what it's trying to say thematically. Almost always, the thought process then goes to rereading it, thinking hard about what it really is, what it means to me, and why it is important for me to have people read this or possibly make it. That kind of enlightens the piece in some ways.

This thing I just finished, it's a true story that's somewhat episodic. It's five days post-Katrina, one guy's story, just a single Katrina story, and all the stuff that happened is beyond belief, terrifying, exciting, funny, and wild. I finished the draft, and it moves like a freight train. I think it's great, but I think, "What's wrong with this? What's missing?" I kept thinking, "What is this really about?" It's a relationship between a man and a lover he shouldn't be with. This is a love story about this guy and his hometown. She keeps looking back, and he's better off without her, and he knows that, but he can't leave her in this time of distress. That kind of informed it for me in a way. I thought that these few days, traveling around the neighborhood, everything now underwater, the memories and flashbacks, and things like that are about this romance with a hometown, so it became about hometowns. Then that helped push me through another draft that became far more complete.

Once that happens, I have two or three people that I will give a script to—if they're not working on their own at the time or they're not too busy—that, one, are really bright and can figure things out or tell you what they think is right or wrong with it, and two, more importantly, have your best interest at heart. That's the hard part to find. I have friends that are screenwriters that are really talented, but I'm not 100% sure they have my best interest at heart. They're great people. Don't get me wrong. But there are a handful of people that, in the past I've given a script to them, and they've given me the good notes—"Yeah, that's great, but let's not talk about that. Here's the stuff that doesn't work. Yeah, you're a good writer, but who cares, let's get to the stuff that doesn't work." It's invaluable.

I find that I'm writing a sequence, and it takes forever, and I don't know why it takes me longer than it used to. It just takes forever, and I'm writing and writing and writing, and I'm thinking, "God, this is so boring." Then I go back the next day and read it, and it takes 32 seconds to read it. It takes hours to write it and 32 seconds to read it, and you start to see for the first time, "Oh, in the movie this could be really fast, just like I had intended." Your experience of doing the thing is completely disjunctive with what it's going to be on screen. I've been writing for so long, but I don't know anything, and that is the key. That is the key to writing. You just don't seem to learn anything. ★ LAWRENCE KASDAN (*Body Heat, Raiders of the Lost Ark*)

Sacha Gervasi on
Getting Started

As a writer working in Hollywood, I am very lucky I came out of film school and was able to start working. The development process, at times, can be a little frustrating. I found myself in notes meetings just going, "Oh, my gosh." Sometimes you're fortunate, and you have someone who is brilliant who is helping you out and really has the same vision. Other times, people are not necessarily so helpful. I was finding myself stuck in the notes process, so I decided to just pick up a camera and make a film. I was a screenwriter who became a director just because, "Why not?"

I picked up a camera and for two years followed some childhood friends of mine called Lips and Robb who formed a very famous band called Anvil. If you're into heavy metal, Anvil actually started the speed metal movement. When I was fifteen I went on the road with them, and I'd lost touch for twenty years and caught back up with them four years ago, and these guys who had influenced all these mega bands like Metallica were still going. The only difference was, they'd never made it. They'd been doing it for 35 years, and they were working in an industrial kitchen in Toronto still believing their moment would come. It struck me that this was kind of like *Rocky*, and I grabbed my camera and went and made this movie on the fly while I was doing assignments and stuff. It was just a magical thing. I didn't care what happened. I just knew I had to make the film, and it was a very powerful experience.

As a writer, you're very lucky that if one script doesn't work out you can write another one. If you really want to make a film, particularly these days, you can just pick up a camera and go make one. That was a hugely liberating thing. I don't have to wait for people to give me permission to do it. I can just go do it. You open the door, and you hope that something good will happen. You have to trust your gut feeling. We shot for two and a half years, and *Anvil* came out reasonably good, but it was really crazy and risky.

I don't think I've ever written on the first page, "This is based on a true story." I can remember having the conversation with people, "I don't want to put that at the beginning," not because it's not true, but because I think it puts your audience in a certain mindset that they don't need to have. If the film is not dramatic and doesn't work on its own, whether you say it's based on a true story or not isn't going to help. Frankly, when I see it on a film, I sometimes think, "Oh, God." It's an excuse to kind of not do it right and try to get away with it by just saying, "That's the way it happened, so if you don't like how it's going . . ." Even though it's true, the structure and the way I approach it is the same as it would be with a fictional story, in terms of the dramatic underpinnings of it. ★ STEVEN ZAILLIAN (*Gangs of New York, Schindler's List*)

The Basics with
Nicholas Kazan

On Planning

You have to plan. You have to have some idea of what you're going to write. Or at least I do. I think when my work is good, it's because I'm closing my eyes and seeing things. I'm typing dialogue so fast that I can barely keep up with myself. Of course later I have to come back and pare it down so that it's economical. But that's how I work. I see pictures; I hear voices. It sounds like madness—maybe it is—but so far I haven't been institutionalized.

On Constructive Criticism

I don't really believe there's such a thing as constructive criticism. All criticism is destructive. Nonetheless you have to absorb the destruction and use it to improve your screenplay, and that means you have to read between the lines of what people are saying. Your friends who are nice to you may tell you it's interesting that your female protagonist is a certain way, but you really have to look and see whether they're saying something more critical.

But you have to be really careful because what other people give you . . . Let's say people say there's a problem with the female protagonist. If you're a guy, they'll say you don't know how to write women. I like feisty people, so sometimes I'm told my female character is a bitch. I don't understand how people get that, but I realize if you have someone behaving in a feisty fashion and it's played by an actress who your heart goes out to, immediately it doesn't matter how feisty she is. You're going to love her. I picture that kind of person playing the role, so I know the feistiness isn't an issue, but I realize I haven't described the character sufficiently because it's so obvious to me.

You have to be careful of your own precepts, what's obvious to you. In a certain sense, writing is a form of psychoanalysis. You look at yourself, you write a scene, it cracks you up, you think it's hysterically funny, and nobody else gets it. Your job is not only to write but also to sell it. You have to sell it to the reader.

Advice from
Bill Wittliff

I will tell you, before you start your first draft, don't do anything. Don't outline. I'm not one who thinks my way through. I don't outline. I don't want to know what's going to happen. I just trust that some part of me does know. If I know, I lose interest in writing. I want a journey of discovery. How do I know what I think until I see what I say? I just trust that some part of me knows, but it may not know it as well as I'd like. Most people write that way, and I know it's probably a better way to write so you know all the beats, acts one, two, three . . . All that stuff. I couldn't do that and don't do that.

> Don't do proposals. If somebody doesn't respond, chances are you'll never write that screenplay. It may be the story that will cut you loose. You do three pages, and nobody buys. Don't do it. Do it so they can see the movie, but if they reject a proposal, I found . . . I don't know anybody who has done a proposal, been rejected on that proposal, and then gone on and wrote the screenplay. I don't know anybody who's ever done that. I think you're cheating yourself as a writer.

I find for me the best thing to do is to get away from it and do something completely different, and all of a sudden it'll pop. The other thing I do as I go to bed is to make a little movie in my head. I see myself the next morning opening the door, sitting down at my desk, grabbing a pencil, grabbing my paper, and starting to write. I'm making this little movie in my head. All of a sudden I'm writing, and I'm smiling. Basically what I'm doing is, I'm trying to project myself, and then the next morning step into it where

I have solved it. I also tell myself, or my muses, "Guys, I have worked my heinie off all day, and I'm tired. You all work this out and give me the stuff tomorrow morning." I know this sounds silly, but listen, it's anything that works for you.

Researching Your Story

I don't do research before. I write it and just trust. I believe everybody already knows everything. That's why great art works. It's not what it's telling you, it's what it's reminding you that you knew but didn't remember you knew. It's why great art, great music, great poetry, great movies always elicit exactly the same response from the viewer the first time he or she views it. If it's really great stuff, it's one word—"yes." It's because whatever that work is, it elicited a familiarity from the viewer. It's an agreement—"yes." Then later they think about it or talk about it and say, "Why is that great? Why is that good?"

You can always come back with research, which is external stuff. It's not heart stuff. It's not. It's a different thing. But it takes a lot of trust to do it.

Anne Rapp's
Writing Routine

Writing is so lonely. When you are writing and in the story, you have this whole world around you, and it's great because you manipulate it. It is only lonely before and after.

Every writer needs a routine. Routines are crucial. A routine is your best friend. A writer without a routine is like a traveler without a compass, a lamp without a light bulb, a master without a dog. I'm proud to say I have a dead-solid perfect routine and I am happy to share it with you.

I wake up very early every morning, with or without an alarm. (I'm a farm girl, and if the sun's up and I'm not, the day's going to waste!) I pour myself a large cup of coffee and get back into bed, trying not to spill it. I turn on the TV and flip around the early local news shows, masterfully avoiding all mattress commercials. I check out the weather, traffic, and sports scores. These things are important even though I have no intention of going outside all day. (Because I'm going to stay home and write!) Of course I already watched most of the ball games the night before, but highlights are essential. You always catch something you missed.)

At 7 a.m., on my second cup of coffee, I peruse the big-dog news shows—*Good Morning America*, *Today Show*, etc. I try to find the least offensive anchor presenting the least banal segment. The dolphin who saved an entire cruise ship full of people? The department store busted for selling "used" underwear? Carrie Underwood on the Plaza? I settle on the Cajun chef whipping up crawfish etouffee. Now there's something I can sink my teeth into.

At 9 a.m. Regis, Kelly, and Ellen remind me that I need to get to work, so I turn off the TV and crawl out of bed. I pass by my full-length mirror and am immediately reminded of the three bowls of chips and salsa I powered back the night before at Manuel's. Ack. Regret rolls over me like the tidal wave of tequila I consumed along with it, so I put on my workout gear. Sometimes I actually go work out. This takes another couple of hours, but it makes me feel good about myself. When I finish I'm totally ready and fired up to go attack that keyboard and create!

I return home, shower, and get dressed—often into the clothes lying on the chair that I took off the night before. This makes me wonder if I'm part Swedish. I've heard that about the Swedes. I go into my office, sit down at the computer and Google "Swedish Dressing Habits." Then I Google "Genealogy." I've always wanted to do a complete family tree and figure out if I'm related to anyone famous. (The only person of distinction I can actually claim kinship to is Rip Torn, but I tend to brush that under the carpet these days.) It's usually about this time that I feel my first hunger pang of the day. I look at my computer clock, which seems to be stuck on Greenwich Mean Time. I Google "Greenwich Mean Time" and read all about Greenwich, England. Then I remind myself I have to deduct six hours to know the real time. The confusion somehow makes me even hungrier, so I get up and go downstairs.

I look at the kitchen clock and realize it's noon for Christ's sake, and I should've eaten something already. You know what they say about people who skip breakfast—total underachievers. So I make a sandwich. While spreading the mayonnaise on the sourdough I remind myself that it's not mentally healthy to work while you eat. You're supposed to be nice to yourself and sit down at a table and actually eat your meal in peace instead of taking it to your computer and working. Also it's better to not drop crumbs into your keyboard. So I do the right thing—I plop down at my kitchen table.

Sometimes I turn on the TV in the corner to see what's on ESPN. (I think watching TV while you're having a meal is okay.) If *SportsCenter* is on, my meal lasts for a good hour. Sometimes I don't turn on the TV, though, but instead pick up the newspaper. After reading every section and finishing the jumble, I get up, clean the dishes, and wander back upstairs to my computer.

By now it's 1 or 2 p.m. It's usually about this time when I notice the three notes on my desk that I made the day before: A. Pick up cleaning.

B. Need paper towels, soy sauce, nail polish remover. C. Call Lisa. I look at the computer clock. It's 8:30 p.m.! No, wait—8:30 minus six hours equals 2:30. Whew. I look at the notes and realize if I run out to the cleaners and Target right now, right this minute, I can get back before the traffic gets bad. And I can call Lisa from the car. Brilliant. I run a brush through my matted hair, swig some mouthwash, whip out the door, and complete all these tasks with lightning speed. I give myself an A for efficiency because I also manage to fill up with gas, stop by the ATM, make a grocery store run, and swing through Bed Bath & Beyond because my 20%-off coupon expires tomorrow. I find myself back at the keyboard by 4 p.m. A record!

I lean back in my chair, proud of myself, and click open the Final Draft file. My latest screenplay comes up on the screen, and the last page I worked on is conveniently displayed in front of me. I look at the last line of dialogue I typed the day before. Or was it the day before that? Can't remember. Anyway, it's about this time I usually feel my second hunger pang of the day. I look at the computer clock, and this time 10 p.m. doesn't throw me at all. I'm getting used to this GMT thing. But I can't bear listening to my stomach growl so I get up and go downstairs.

I open the fridge and stare at all my food. Since this will be a "snack" and not a "meal," I'm allowed to take it upstairs and munch while I work. I consider apple butter on Triscuits, but I remember I had that yesterday. So I decide on my other favorite—low-calorie meringue. I invented this one myself, although I'm sure others have tried it because it's SO obvious. I crack three eggs, discard the yolks, and put the whites in a bowl. I beat until frothy, add salt, and continue to beat to desired stiffness. Then I add a 50/50 combo of sugar and Splenda. I tried it with all Splenda but it doesn't work. Too not-sweet. When the meringue is the perfect texture I take the bowl upstairs with a spoon. (Yes, raw. I once tried cooking the meringue— like you would on top of a pie but just by itself in a clump. It was like eating caulk.)

I settle back into my chair in front of the computer and eat the meringue while scrolling back a few pages and reading the last work I did on my screenplay. Usually I finish the meringue at about the same time I get to the end—or rather the starting point for today. I put the spoon down and use my finger to lick the bowl clean, really concentrating by now. I'm in the zone, as they say. I put the bowl next to my keyboard and start to really dive in when I realize how sticky my fingers are. And besides, I hate having an empty bowl of anything next to my computer. It distracts me terribly. So I get up and take the bowl downstairs. I wash my hands, look up at the kitchen clock, and notice it's getting close to 5 p.m. My goodness, almost cocktail hour! Where did the day go?

Believe it or not, I actually go back upstairs and sit down at the computer again. But at this point things can go any direction. I guess you could say this is where the routine might start to waver a little bit.

Sometimes I actually do start writing. Although sometimes I write for a short time, then look up and notice it's 5:30 p.m., and I realize I need to watch the national news to make sure nothing important has happened today. And after that I remind myself of the evening schedule on ESPN. Don't want to miss Villanova/Seton Hall. (Note: If it's late March, or Xmas bowl season, none of this applies.)

After lingering on the local 6:30 news to see what the weather is going to do, I shut off the TV, pick up the "sissy" vodka tonic I made a few minutes ago, and turn back toward my computer room. I am stopped in my tracks by the glow of light coming from beneath the door.

I turn to the window, pull the curtain back, and peer outside. And this is when the inevitable occurs. Yes, the inevitable—even if that happens to all the farm girls in all the joints in all the towns in all the world who ever chose to be a writer—the sun goes down! And when the sun goes down you know what that means. Quittin' time! So the computer goes off, and the rest of the night is delegated to rewarding myself for the hard day I've put in.

Lucky for me I have a lot in my life to help with the reward process: Good friends who will join me at the sushi bar. My sports package on Dish. A mountain of *New Yorkers* and fashion magazines mixed together like a shuffled deck of cards on my coffee table. That and a good bottle of red, and there's no way I won't end this day on a high note. I finish off the night with a healthy dose of Jon Stewart and Stephen Colbert, then the clothes come off and go on the chair, and it's lights out. And I drift off to sleep with the comfort of knowing that the rooster will crow early tomorrow morning and I will wake up and thrive again as a writer. Because who is my best friend forever? My dead-solid perfect routine! Every writer should be so fortunate.

Caroline Thompson's
Writing Process

I know over the years one develops one's own system. My system is, I go to my office and write a certain number of pages, five pages to be exact, and then I get to leave. My office is a separate building, not so much a room of my own as a hut of my own, no more glamorous than the neighbor's tool shed I first wrote in when I realized I needed to leave the house to work, otherwise I would find tons of stuff to do all day, tons of distractions that would keep me from writing.

So I go there, and the dog comes with me sometimes so I am not always by myself. I write my five pages. That gets me through the first draft in a month. If I get a blaze of energy and write ten pages, I get exhausted for four days, and I lose my pace. I know I have to pace myself at five pages a day.

I march through the first pass, it usually sucks, but I have gotten there. When I go to work in the morning, I never read what is behind me. I just keep going forward. Afterwards, after I have a pass, I start the process of refining and revising, and usually, for whatever reason, I go through that five times before I show it to anybody. Steve, my husband, is usually the first person I show it to, but not always. Sometimes I just feel like, "Okay, I am ready to give it to them," whoever "them" is.

Lawrence Kasdan on the Challenges of Writing

I have friends who are much more prolific than I am, and I'm very jealous of them. They don't seem to edit as rigorously as I do, and that's not a bad thing. It means they're able to produce more work than me. A lot of times when I'm editing I'll say, "I've seen it before." You could say that about anything because there are only a few stories. "I've done this before myself." That's probably true, because we tend to tell the same story again and again. "I don't like this enough." Those are just three reasons you can use to stop, and once you stop, you've released yourself from the hard work. That's really what you're looking for every minute when you're sitting at the computer—you're looking for an excuse not to be doing it.

I find writing to be hard work, and my reaction to all hard things is to turn away. Hard work is easy to turn away from, especially if you have an excuse. The unreliable narrator in your head will say, "This isn't any good. I should quit this. I have this other idea that seems really good right now." In fact, some people are able to channel that attraction to the other idea into real work. One of the guys I was reading said he always has more than one thing going for that very reason. It's always more attractive to turn away, but sometimes if you turn away, you'll want to come back to it. So you may say, "This is my escape hatch, and I'm just going to use it to get out of doing this," or you may actually be on to something, and the story is not good enough.

It may not be good enough because there's no inherent conflict in it. It may not be good enough because it's so familiar that you've only moved it five degrees away from stories you've seen a hundred times, and five degrees is not good enough. It may not be good enough because it bores you after 25 pages. So there are actually some stories you're shying away from not just to get out of the work, but because they're not good enough. That's the job, unfortunately, sorting out which ones are worth investing your time in and which ones aren't. It takes a lot of blood and sweat, and if you aren't being paid for it, which covers 99.9% of screenwriting in the world, then finding the motivation is hard.

The truth is, you're writing all the time. If your purpose is to tell stories, there's some part of you that's working on stories all the time. One of the great things about writing, you're writing alone, and you kind of disappear into it. I would assume, but for sure would hope, that all of you have gotten to the point where you absolutely disappear into your own writing. The best possible thing in the world is to look down at what you wrote in the last hour or so and say, "My God, I didn't know I knew that." What a miraculous thing. We all have that. Have faith in that. We're all little gods.

★ BILL WITTLIFF (*The Black Stallion, Lonesome Dove*)

4

Structure

Tootsie was a script that I turned down at least six times. Because I thought it was a terrible script, and initially it was. Although there were a lot of jokes, it was the same joke. The problem with *Tootsie*, in its initial stages, it was a one-joke movie.

What can this movie be about that can give us some sort of spine, some sort of rudder that shapes the movie, so that it . . . people change in it. What happens to the people? What is the closure? What is illuminated? What is it about? There was a line that Larry [Gelbart] wrote, where the character of the agent says, "Being a woman has made you weird, Michael." And it suddenly occurred to me that if that line was, "Being a woman has made a man out of you," that we would have something to make the movie about. ★ SYDNEY POLLACK (director, *Tootsie*, *Out of Africa*)

Structure and Format

A Conversation with Frank Pierson, Whit Stillman,
Robin Swicord, and Nicholas Kazan

On Structure

FRANK PIERSON: I've been writing for many years and discovered that it's no easier now than when I started. Structure is everything.

WHIT STILLMAN: I don't think structure is everything.

ROBIN SWICORD: I've been writing screenplays and selling them since about 1979. It took me a very long time to begin to understand structure, and it did not, for me, come from the outside. It came from the inside. I learned to understand it from the inside. So I would say that books are not everything, but I also agree with Frank that structure is everything, as long as it comes out of character. It's actually character that's everything.

NICHOLAS KAZAN: I'll just say mystery is everything. What I mean by that is, in a movie or in any narrative or dramatic form, the audience wants to know that the writer has a secret, and the audience wants to know what that is. Sometimes there are many secrets. What propels a story forward is the audience's desire to know.

When you write, you have to structure narrative information so that the audience gets it in little pieces and finds out a little bit more about what they want to know but doesn't find out everything. At the point where the audience knows everything they want to know, whether you know it or not, your movie is over.

You don't have to structure as Syd Field does or as any of us do. You can structure in your own way as long as you are sustaining a mystery and the audience is compelled to continue to watch. You have some form of narrative structure, and that's all you need.

PIERSON: I think there is certainly confusion about what structure actually is. The idea that there is an intellectual organization of the material . . .

Everything in the movie is planned. There's not a line of dialogue, nothing an actor does, nothing that a director does that is not planned for an effect or is not put in there for a very specific reason. If you take it out or you change it, you've got to look at everything else in the screenplay for what is altered because everything else changes, and what it means changes when you take anything significant out.

On Screenwriting Books and Courses

STILLMAN: I think when we set out to become screenwriters we go through an educational process. I arrived at it much later than everyone here. Syd Field's book was already out, and as someone with no confidence, you approach these books or these courses, and I think some courses are sort of basically good. Some seem much less good. There's a lot of potentially destructive stuff in the courses too.

I think it'd be interesting to know if you all have an opinion about each teacher or each sort of spokesperson, how much good and bad is there. I was talking to a guy who produced a screenplay, and he said the McKee course is good, but after he took it, he wrote terrible stuff for eight months. I think a lot of the stuff exemplifies the huge difference between the conscious process of talking or thinking about screenwriting and actually creating.

When you are creating a screenplay, you're diving into a place that is not very conscious. It's dipping into some sort of morass, and you have to come up with stuff. Once you've come up with a lot of stuff, you can start structuring, moving around, and keeping up the tension and mystery. If you just think in terms of what these teachers say, you get no living story.

I don't know how many of us have taken the McKee course, but it's a lot of money. It's a big thing if you lose eight months of writing time after taking it, because that's part of your life.

SWICORD: I haven't taken the McKee course. When I was a beginning screenwriter, I went to a Syd Field weekend . . . I think it was a three-day thing. I went for one day. I didn't go to the next two days.

STILLMAN: Did you get a refund?

SWICORD: I wasn't aggressive enough to get my refund, but I had his book, and as I looked at it, I felt that what was wrong with the book and with a lot of structure courses is that someone stands up there and says, "Now, this is the way! You've got to know this plot point by Thursday! And this plot point happens here!" There's very little discovery that's allowed.

I mentored a beginning screenwriter, a woman who had written novels, poetry, and short stories. She had done her graduate work in literature. She was a really erudite woman with a lot of gifts toward writing prose. She was interested in screenwriting, and my suggestion to her was, "Why don't you adapt something, because then the story is there and you're not quite so afloat." So she found a book to adapt. I helped her to analyze it: This movement makes that movement, and that movement makes this. Once we had talked through her ideas, she went away to write.

Her first draft was really interesting, but it kind of sprawled. As she continued to refine it, I saw it getting better and more like a movie, less like a novel. Then she took McKee's course, and the piece of work she gave me after taking McKee's course was unreadable. Not only was it not dramatic, but also the things that had been beautiful in her writing, eccentric characters and choices we didn't understand in the moment but would understand later, had been ironed out. It was flat. There was nothing in it, no life in it.

That's why I said it has to come out of character. You're hearing voices. You're thinking about subjects. Thematic concerns begin to come up. You think about how you're organizing it into a story, but it comes from a person who is in the situation. Because of that, then this, and because of that, then that, and the story emerges.

When you come at it with a grid and say that by page 30 you've got to have a turning point and by page 5 you've got to have an inciting incident, you're getting locked into a kind of thing. It is not an algebraic equation. You have to find your story, and it's a kind of mystery, unfolding in a certain way, and subplots have to connect and push other things, but beyond that, the idea that one person can stand up there and tell you exactly how your personal screenplay is supposed to go is absurd.

For me it's useful to have my own private schematic, my own private way of kind of making a picture of it on the page in words, so that I'm organizing my own thoughts.

KAZAN: With an outline?

SWICORD: It's sort of like an outline. It helps me know how long the story is, because when I first started writing, I knew so little about structure that I can't even imagine what got into my head that made me think I could write a movie. I don't think I even understood what a movie was when I wrote my first screenplay, which by some incredible miracle was actually sold. It was as if I had gone up on a high wire and was expected to walk it. I didn't have a clue about how to do it. People were listening to me in meetings as if I knew what I was talking about. I was in a state of terror.

So I had to develop my own way of thinking about it on a page so I could go in and talk to them. Try to understand what a story is, and then you get inside, and then you can be your own Robert McKee.

KAZAN: The problem with these courses is, they analyze and dissect. They say all good movies have certain characteristics, and they can show you exactly, but if you try to create from that place, you can't do it. You can look at it as you're outlining and use these things as constructs, but when you're writing, you have to throw it away. I don't use any of these structural templates. As far as I'm concerned, they are of no value. You have movies inside you. If you're writing movies, it's because you love movies. If you love movies, you carry the rhythm of movies inside you.

At the beginning of the movie you want something to happen. Otherwise, why are you sitting there watching? You're bored. If nothing happens in fifteen minutes, you're going to walk out. You don't need to be told there's got to be an inciting incident. You start a movie, something should happen. The sooner it happens, the better, although you have a grace period with the audience while they're getting into the world of the movie, and if what they're seeing is entertaining, you can get away without having the incident.

My advice is, if you want to use these books, fine. Use them before or after you do a draft if there's something wrong with it, but if you try to fit . . . Are you really going to stop in the middle and say, "No, wait a second. I want to check this with Syd Field"? It's creation. Writing or creating something is the same as making love. It's an act of God if it goes well. If it goes badly . . . The one thing that can ensure you're not really making love is if you're checking the book in the middle to see how you're doing.

Character Arcs

SWICORD: In terms of the studio executives, it is one of the more horrifying things to sit in a meeting and have somebody who's never written a screenplay tell you that something isn't working because you need . . . And then they supply a buzzword. Everybody gets infected with it. It isn't just studio executives.

One of the things they talk about a lot in a story is the character arc.

Your character's got to change—unless what's unique about this character is that she doesn't change. There's always something that you're doing that's not by the book. In *Little Women*, the character Marmee is the universe upon which this entire family stands, and the whole thing about Marmee is that she is immutable. She does not change. She is this mother who is their world, their platform, and from her these young women can now be ambitious and go out and have their lives.

There was a moment when Susan Sarandon said, "My character doesn't change. What's my character arc?" We were able to fudge our way out of that, but the whole thinking that there's something wrong unless it follows somebody else's construct is dangerous to the work. That is one of the reasons we see cookie-cutter scripts.

PIERSON: What you just said is interesting to me because you have somebody, in this case an actress, not a studio executive, and she's saying, "What am I doing? What is my job here? Usually when I play a part, don't I have a place where I start, and then something happens, and I arrive at a different place than I would've expected?" And you're telling her that the interesting thing about the character is that she doesn't change.

But that gives you a clue as to how you go about structuring the writing of that character. You're trying to constantly confront her with situations that demand that she change and adjust. Other characters bring pressure to bear on her to make her change, and she doesn't. The drama grows out of the fact that they're frustrated with her because she doesn't . . .

SWICORD: If that's what it's about.

PIERSON: If that's what it's about. So often we're confronted with a scene that doesn't work. In the earlier years of my career I depended upon a book by a Hungarian named Lajos Egri called *The Art of Dramatic Writing*, which I think still is the best book in this field because it's not so page-by-page structurally organized. It has much more to do with how you conceive of a character, what a scene is about, and so on.

Conflict was the major thing. I used to have this huge sign over my typewriter that said, "Conflict, Stupid." Nine times out of ten if you've got a scene that's not working for some reason, the characters are not in conflict. They're just giving out information. They're wandering around and not going anywhere.

As we were talking it reminded me of Flannery O'Connor's famous remark that, "Yes, we believe in a beginning, a middle, and an end in storytelling, but not necessarily in that order."

KAZAN: I was reminded of something else. I wrote a film called *Reversal* • *of Fortune*, and we realized partway through the production that none of the central characters changed. And yet we hear that all characters must change, and certainly your main character must change. None of the characters changed, and yet the movie was satisfying because there were a lot of mysteries that were resolved during the film. We used to joke during the production that American movies are sustained by the illusion that human beings are capable of change. Usually we're not. In a story it's better if your characters do change. It makes the drama a little more satisfying, but it's not necessary.

PIERSON: One of the great dramas of Western dramaturgy is a play in which nobody changes and nothing happens—*Waiting for Godot*.

KAZAN: That's right. Absolutely. A masterpiece.

Waiting for Godot and Lack of Structure

PIERSON: *Waiting for Godot* is a play that defies all those Syd Field and Lajos Egri rules.

SWICORD: But it's not a screenplay.

PIERSON: It's not a screenplay, but the two disciplines are related, except one is telling stories in terms of action and the other primarily with words. Their structures are very strongly related. *Waiting for Godot* appears to have no structure at all, but it has a steely discipline that is absolutely arresting. You know that it took a mind that was enormously disciplined and focused to write that. That's what you're perceiving on stage, and it's a lot of where the drama comes from.

STILLMAN: I think that essentially what Nick was saying is right, that starting out you have to go somewhere very deep and get characters who begin to speak with a tone of voice and start creating the reality of a fictional world. You've got to go into that fictional world and hope there's forward momentum and a story happening that's interesting. When you come back to look at what you've done, or get stuck not liking your draft, then I think some of this advice is helpful. It helps one analyze and think about one's predicament.

Some have described *Metropolitan* as meandering. That's good, I think; the good part of *Metropolitan* is the meandering. Before we cut a lot out, it was not so much meandering as static. Material that seemed interesting or funny on the printed page, long speeches by the actor Taylor Nichols, the preppy Spengler, the philosopher of doom. Everyone seemed to like these at the script stage but Taylor had a nose for what wouldn't quite work. I couldn't believe he wasn't thrilled with everything in the part. It all seemed so "interesting" to us. Why wasn't he as thrilled?

He kept focusing on the second half of the movie when his character, Charlie, gets to be friends with the protagonist and they become an odd pairing going off in search of the heroine to "rescue" her. I wish I had listened to Taylor before I shot the film because when we were in the editing room, the long speeches about sociology that were funny theoretically were just deadly. The film just stopped. Whenever it was building up—in a meandering way, of course—toward relationships of the characters, leading to something that later could pay off, it worked far better.

With *Barcelona*, I had a scene, a sort of recapitulation scene toward the end of the movie after a hospital sequence, after a lot of things happened, and Taylor asked, "Do we really need to do this scene?"

I said, "Definitely. We have to do this. They won't understand what's happening." We cut it out at the end. Taylor, had I listened to his advice, would have saved us lots of money. Time and again when I see the films with audiences and I see restlessness or a lull, I do think that some of the things Syd Field or Robert McKee say could've been useful. I think you have to have a lot of integrity about your own work and what you're creating and reject all the stuff they're saying that's formulaic or unhelpful. Be really selective about what you pick and choose to use. But it can be a sort of medical test to check what's not working in your story.

Even the kind of films that someone's going to make that are less overtly mainstream, they have to be going somewhere. There can be a meandering approach if it's finally arriving somewhere, because the audience is surprised—"Gosh, this film actually arrived somewhere. I thought we were going nowhere with this."

PIERSON: I think the word "meander" is an interesting word because it implies a search for something. You're in motion. Your characters are seeking some truth. That's the mystery.

STILLMAN: The audience likes to be surprised, and if they think they're just meandering and suddenly they come to a fountain, that's a positive thing for them.

KAZAN: Character can also come from plot. That is, if you want to write a story about a man who kills his mother, you have to create a character who could realistically do that. You can't say, "I'm going to write a story about a man who kills his mother, and I just love my Uncle George, so I'm going to base it on my Uncle George because that's a fantastic character." Uncle George might be someone who would never murder his mother, so it's not believable. You have to create someone who will serve your functions. They're hand in hand. You can't have one ever without the other.

SWICORD: Yes, you can. I had a feeling you were getting at a certain kind of genre picture in which character is less important than plot. One that comes to mind is *Speed*. All we need to know about Keanu Reeves is that he doesn't want people to die. It's true that Sandra Bullock's likability and realness help the audience in an unreal situation, but the movie didn't come out of her. In fact, by act three she's an object. They've got bombs strapped to her, and she's just a thing that needs to be rescued. That bus was driving her. She was not driving that bus.

What I gathered from Nick is that you can't have people doing things that they're not psychologically prepared for. In some films we come to understand the hero—in this case Officer Jack Traven—doesn't say much, which in this film is kind of a blessing. All we had to know was that he was heroic, as opposed to something like *Lethal Weapon*, where you had a man who was crazy and would do and say anything—Mel Gibson—so you're waiting for that next surprise. He's played off a family man who's much more stodgy. And so even though there was a very tightly imposed action-genre structure—this has got to happen, that has got to happen, the bad guys are here—you had these people playing off each other. We felt in some way that the insanity that was happening was also coming out of Mel Gibson, whereas basically Keanu and the woman driving the bus were reacting to the situation that they were in, and the stakes were always being raised by somebody else.

PIERSON: The Hollywood king of the unstructured movie supposedly is Bob Altman. I happen to disagree with that. I think that *Nashville* is one of the most tightly structured movies ever made, brilliantly choreographed by an ex-choreographer who became a writer, Joan Tewkesbury. In fact, she drew diagrams of the action and the interrelating of how we get from this to that and so on. The movements appear to be random, but they are tied together by some sort of autosuggestion on her part. To what extent were those characters driving that story?

SWICORD: They were. There's always the exception that proves the rule. In that case, I feel those characters were so loopy, and they all contributed to the story. Writing for an ensemble is a separate thing in terms of structure. I've written a lot of ensemble movies. In fact, I've never had a movie made that was not an ensemble picture. When you're working with an ensemble, a lot of smaller questions make up the larger narrative. It's like you're drawing a line from each one of those characters, and together they are creating this beautiful world. It's like a dance, a tapestry, where you see these things come together into one.

PIERSON: I think the real problem is that there is no single structural model or paradigm that fits every possible movie you might want to go see. I think that movies are all very structured. I think that in all the movies that are of any value you can go in and tease out the structure. Sometimes it's not quite as obvious as it is in the case of a thriller or something like that. I think that the difficulty in trying to think about structure in the McKee/Syd Field kind of way is you tend to take one simple formula and try to apply it to everything, and it doesn't work.

Lawrence of Arabia

PIERSON: A major problem with the movie is that he goes through these agonies out in the desert and all the rest, and then he reaches a point where he's been raped by what's-his-name who played the Turk, José Ferrer. I guess some people might like to be raped by José Ferrer, but he didn't like it.

STILLMAN: He said he didn't like it.

PIERSON: In any case, the very premise of the movie is, here is a man who has fallen in love with the primitivism and the noble savages, and he thinks he can find his salvation in the desert, but he discovers that they're all being betrayed by the government he's working for, and there's nothing left for him in the desert, so he goes home to England. We dissolve, and he's right back there in Allenby's office saying, "I'm ready to go back to war again." You never see what happens in England.

SWICORD: Yeah.

PIERSON: They left that out. The movie works okay without it, but I think it was a failure of their imagination that they could not think of what it was that happened in England that would be interesting enough to keep in the picture.

KAZAN: I agree completely. I'm not a big fan of that movie. I felt that absence, and it really hurt the movie for me. One of the things that's critical to movie construction is that you leave things out. Usually, you don't leave out something so big, but in a sense, there's a mystery lurking in that movie, which is what happened in that section, and it kind of pervades the movie. You feel it as you're coming to it, and you feel it afterward, and there's kind of a sense of never really completely knowing another human being, never really knowing the hero. That's very central to the conception of that movie, so the movie actually gets some energy out of its flaw.

PIERSON: You think that's what Bolt said to Lean to explain why they were leaving that scene out? Did you ever see *Papillon*, the picture with Dustin Hoffman and . . .?

SWICORD: Steve McQueen.

PIERSON: They're escaping from the world's worst hell, and they're going through jungle or one thing or the other, and finally around the middle of the movie, they reach this absolute paradise of a native village. For the first time in the movie you have kind of a rift, and they're being fed and massaged, and their wounds are being healed. These people are peaceful, wonderful people and all the rest of it. Then when they leave that and go on through the jungle and so on, they have a lot of horrible further adventures, and they know that even if they get back, their friends are probably just going to be captured and put back in jail again and so on.

So in the course of writing the picture, somebody asked a very intelligent question—"Why would they ever leave this village? Why on earth?" Suddenly, everything stopped, and for literally a week or so, they did nothing but try to invent what would happen in this village that would lead them to leave.

Finally, Frank Schaffner, the director, said nothing should happen there. What happens is, just at the moment they're saying, "My God, this is wonderful," and so on, they wake up one morning, and all the villagers have gone, just disappeared. They are terrified because they think, "My God, they must know something terrible is going to happen," and that's why they leave and continue into the jungle.

SWICORD: So it's mysterious again.

PIERSON: Yes. It's a mystery, a brilliant conception.

SWICORD: It was brilliant.

Character Milestones

KAZAN: There are a couple of things I look for as kind of milestones. There is a critical thing that happens early on. When you first begin a story—

sometimes it happens right away, right in the very first frame—there is a point at which a character is being confronted with other characters in conflict with him or a situation he can't resolve or what have you. There is a point at which, if he just simply stops and decides whatever it is he wanted in the picture is not worth it, he can always get back to the life he led before. So I look for that moment when something happens, and mostly I want it to happen because the character—it grows out of the character's qualities and the nature of the man or the woman—does something that pushes him past the point of no return. From that point on, he can never get his old life back. He has to go forward into unknown territory.

For the middle part of the movie, it's exploring in various ways, "I'm now confronted with this situation. I can't go back to my old life. I can't get whatever it is I want, and maybe I don't even know what it is that I'm trying to find or achieve." He's making all these choices, and the other characters in the piece are reacting to those choices. His direction begins to slowly emerge.

The second major turning point for me is the point at which it becomes clear what the final choice is. That's the "third act." But the movie never stops. It just goes continually on through, so I don't like to think in terms of act structure.

SWICORD: But it is like three movements. It does happen in three movements.

KAZAN: But it's more like music than it is like . . .

SWICORD: It is. It's much more like music than what we think of as play structure.

Notes from the Studio

PIERSON: When you're talking to studio executives, they may say, "Page thirteen, can't we have something here? Why doesn't she do this? I don't like him because he says that." I don't take anything they say at face value. I don't want to hear it. If it gets too hot and heavy, I try to say as politely as I feel at the moment, "Look, you're paying me a lot of money to do this, so don't tell me how to do it, because if you know how then just get a stenographer in here if you want to dictate it." But what I'm listening for is that something is bothering them. They're bored at that moment. They don't understand it, and if they don't, that's what I need to address. I need to try to determine for myself why it is they feel that way.

KAZAN: Sometimes they'll tell you that the second act is slow whereas actually the first act is slow, and they start to feel it too late. If you tighten up the first act, the second act plays fine. You have to diagnose. You have to be like a doctor diagnosing what they tell you. What they tell you are symptoms.

STILLMAN: I remember that in book publishing we were much more inclined to buy a proposal on three chapters and an outline than a finished book because with three chapters and an outline you can imagine this wonderful thing. If it's already finished, it's such a downer. It's not what you imagined. I think that within 20 to 30 pages there should be enough mystery created that . . . What I don't like really is an outline that reveals the entire story—your bad and unoriginal early ideas become an albatross it's nearly impossible for you to escape from. Why not send 30 pages and say, "If you want to see what comes later, ask me, and I'll send you the rest"?

PIERSON: In terms of working in Hollywood—I don't know about the film festival scene and that kind of thing particularly—certainly the first draft that I turn in to the studio has a lot more in it than it's going to have when we actually get down to the production rewrite. That's because a lot of the people at the studio who are going to read it are only going to read it one time, but they're the ones who make the decision as to whether they're going to push it ahead. They're not very good at reading screenplays, and they're not particularly imaginative.

A lot of directors are not very good at reading. Some of them are barely literate, even major directors. I'm quite serious about this, by the way. They just don't know how to read. The words on the page don't compute. So you have to give them a considerable amount more information than you want to. By the time I've gotten a screenplay—if I'm writing for myself to direct—ready to work with the actors on it, I'll have cut out a lot of dialogue that I put in originally to be sure that everybody at the studio got the point. Also, of course, you have to take . . . If you're working for another director, when he comes on board you have to take out all the shot directions, because they hate that.

SWICORD: The very first screenplay I sold, people came to me as I was doing it and said, "We can't give this to directors until you take a lot of stuff out, because the directors will be insulted if you say, 'She's wearing a blue dress.' You have to just say, 'She walks into a room.'" So my second draft of the screenplay was really flat. I tried not to describe anything or reveal too much so that the director would have some room to come in and do what they needed to do. It was a really big mistake, and I really felt that I was writing in a straitjacket.

We are storytellers. Page one: This is what the room looks like. This is what the weather is. This person comes in, and something happens here. We don't know who that person is yet, but you're going to find out by the end of page two exactly who that person is, because they're either going to show you or tell you. You have to make it really immediate. It is written in the present tense. You have to communicate what you are seeing in your head, and you can't do that by writing big blocks. You have to find a way to tell it really concisely and quickly so they don't forget, and so it makes a really strong impression on them.

People like the Sundance workshops. We were just at the Sundance Screenwriters Lab, where I saw scripts in which I couldn't believe the workshop people would let this person in, purely on the basis of their writing. What the Sundance staff was responding to in some of these cases was that the artist had already made a film or something, and the workshop people could see that this person had a lot of talent, but wasn't a writer yet. So they were bringing him to this lab to show him . . . maybe somebody who had really interesting characters and no sense of structure at all, but what they were writing was very lively on the page. There was a life happening there. And I guess that was what hooked the Sundance people.

I don't think in these workshops they're looking for someone who is a mint-perfect writer—"Boy, this person really knows how to write, so we're going to invite him." There's something else that jumps off the page at them, and I think the thing that jumps off the page is you.

Taboo Topics

PIERSON: Religion. Forget it. Nobody in Hollywood believes in God. They also don't understand the religious experience or the religious impulse.

SWICORD: In film that's a signifier for crazy, in fact, right?

PIERSON: Yeah.

KAZAN: *Radio Flyer* was a spec script that sold for a lot of money. I guess it made a bad movie. I didn't see it. It was about child abuse. That would normally be considered a taboo subject. If you write about that, you would have to handle it in exactly the right way, and at least as a writer he handled it in a fairly effective way apparently. I never read the script. It all depends on how you do it.

PIERSON: Slavery is another unmarketable subject in Hollywood. They do not want to do pictures about slavery. There are very fine screenplays out there that have been floating around for years that major directors have wanted to do on various slave revolts or the slave experience and so on. They don't want to do them.

Workshopping a Script

SWICORD: I get as much as I can stand. I like for Nick to read my scripts because Nick and I are married, so that's easy—someone who lives in your house who can read your script. But I find there are things I'm insecure about when I've finished that Nick doesn't necessarily focus on, so it's helpful for me when I can give it to somebody else that I work with. If I get too much input I find it to be destructive. In fact, I look at these writers who go through the Sundance thing, or any other similar workshop, they may have a meeting on their one poor little script with twelve different people in four days. Personally, if I were that writer, I would want to kill myself—because you can't possibly know at the end of that time what you want to change in the work. What you would be left with is, "What I've written is nothing. It's just something these people have thrown their egos up against." How you reclaim your script and make it your own again must be quite a process.

PIERSON: Robin is so right about Sundance. You have twelve instructors and the writers, and once a day the teachers, or whatever we call ourselves, all meet and discuss the problems we perceive in each one of these screenplays. The unanimity is wonderful. Everybody agrees about what the problems are, which is very reassuring. It indicates there is some science and method in the whole thing. But then you talk to the twelve people—all experienced and all the rest of it—about how to solve the problems, and they all go off in wildly different directions, which is also very reassuring because it indicates there is an art to screenwriting.

You can't assume that just because somebody has an idea about your screenplay that they're smarter than you are. You know your screenplay. What you need to do is say, "Well, why did they have that idea?" Maybe that triggers something else that comes from inside you.

KAZAN: I show my scripts to one person, and then I get a response, and I do some work. Then I show it to another person. Sometimes I'll spend a day reacting to comments, or I'll spend a week or two reacting, and I keep going. Sometimes I will disregard a comment and say, "I don't agree with that." If I don't agree with it, I will dismiss it out of hand. But if the second and third readers say the same thing, you know you've got a genuine problem that you've got to pay attention to.

I find it invaluable to do that. You can't take anyone's opinion to heart. Only respond to things that have resonance inside you. But once you hear something for the third time, it starts to have resonance inside you. You have to deal with it. But do it your own way. Don't pay attention to anybody else.

On the Format of a Script

SWICORD: It has to look professional and be easy to read. What's hard to read is, "He is running," and then, "She is doing that," and after a while you're wondering why they can't just say, "He runs," and "She runs," in the present tense without being too crazy about it. Just try to make it easy for the eye to run down the page and understand what the story is.

PIERSON: The big mistake is writing inner dialogue, the thoughts of the character, the stage direction that says, "He comes out of the building looking like he wants to make a telephone call."

STILLMAN: I think that's superb. I like that. There isn't an "I want to make a call" look.

SWICORD: When a character has a really big realization and it's supposed to be conveyed merely with an expression on their face, it is difficult to know how to convey it simply, without dialogue. Apropos to what you were saying about putting more on the page than will be there in the end— you can't believe what readers don't get when they're reading your screenplay. So I have started putting the character's inner thoughts in the screen directions, here and there. I put it in, underlined, so the direction reads, "He looks at her," and then I write what this man is thinking, his specific thought, because that thought gives us an expression you can read on the actor's face. There are a lot of, "He looks at her incredulously," or whatever. Is it disbelief at the absurdity of the situation? Is it disbelieving joy? If you can give the reader the specific and it works to clarify the moment, it doesn't look like you're padding your screenplay. It's a signpost for the reader, because they may not know that when he looks at her incredulously he's on the verge of making a decision. That subtlety may go past them.

PIERSON: Well, you can do that with the little parentheses under the character's name.

STILLMAN: That's what Nick does.

PIERSON: I call them "wrylys" because, more often than not, that's what's under the character's name—"wryly."

STILLMAN: Right.

PIERSON: I always know where I'm trying to get, but I often don't know where I'm going to start. I have to go back and start, and then I go sequentially and try to make an outline, which is just sort of a general idea of how I'm going to get to that ending place. Then every three days or so I take another look at that outline, and I have to throw it out because it's been completely changed. So I know what the next few scenes I'm going to write are, but I have to go sequentially all the way through, one foot in front of the other, then two steps backward, and falling down stairs, and climbing back and forth, and all that.

STILLMAN: A lot of times we go through the whole process, and only when you get to the end of filmmaking do you do something that's very creative and very exciting that maybe you could've done a lot earlier. When you're in production and in the editing room you tend to start throwing away stuff—"We don't have time for this." You're just so delighted to get rid of some stuff that's not playing well in the screenings.

I think that now that I'm thinking about this in the script stage it would be an interesting exercise to take stuff out of your script that you think is essential and go through it without that and see if you're not adding a new dimension to it, adding on to it. One thing that I think is very bad about a lot of the advice books and courses is the way they try to denigrate dialogue. I know what they're responding to, because a lot of people just think dialogue will cover all of this, and their scripts are just dialogue, and it's not heading anywhere. But even in action films sometimes there's absolutely great dialogue that makes them incredibly popular and fun to watch, and it's very funny and very true to character. Dialogue is so much the personality of the character of the movie, and this sort of rogue thing of saying dialogue is unimportant is just nonsense.

PIERSON: "Go ahead. Make my day."

STILLMAN: Another thing that's negative about the courses and the books is, you get this idea, "I have to have the motivation for the character," and the motivation becomes kind of this awful stone, a motif that goes through the whole movie that no one cares about. I remember in the film *A Few Good Men*, the character point for Tom Cruise's character is that his father was some great lawyer or judge, and the story keeps coming back to his insecurity, because his father was such a great lawyer. We've gotten so familiar with this sort of Motivation 101 and inured to it. We know all about that kind of stuff, and that's the most boring part of that film.

At another film screening I couldn't help noticing that the two people who most liked the film were those who had arrived twenty minutes late. They missed the scene where the inciting crime was committed. And the rest of the film became much more interesting for them than for everyone else as they had to use their imagination to figure out what might have happened. So maybe it would be a good idea to consider removing the first thirty pages of your script. Let them guess what happened.

Recommended Reading

STILLMAN: I'd like to give my reading list because there were some things that seemed terribly helpful. One is a book of interviews with screenwriters called *The Craft of the Screenwriter* by John Brady. He does a really wonderful interview, and there are five terrific screenwriters he interviewed on the craft of screenwriting.

I thought the screenplay for *The Big Chill*, which they printed in a facsimile version, was very helpful. I didn't know screenplay format and this was a case of good form and brilliant content. Also *The Big Chill* is a beautifully told ensemble story dealing with the issues that really do face us and our peers.

Another really interesting book—though I'm not sure how directly useful it is—is *Five Screenplays by Preston Sturges*. I'm not certain if Preston Sturges's screenplays are that relevant to the kind of screenplays someone would write now, but the book is terribly good. It has a long piece about the genesis of each screenplay, and how many years it took, and the different drafts, and what was left in and left out.

In reading Preston Sturges's biography, he taught himself with a book that was popular in those days on dramatic structure in playwriting by Brander Matthews. He keeps saying how he's reading each chapter of Brander Matthews and writing his plays, which later became the genesis for some of the great movies he made in the '40s. I think there's a lot of value almost indirectly from these books. They suggest things to you.

When you get a good book the stimulation effect is terrific. You have your coffee breaks, you're working on something, you read half of it, and you get so many great ideas from reading about other people and their problems. I think that's totally useful.

There's another book with a series of interviews, and it's incredible how useful some of the interviews are. There's one with Nunnally Johnson, one with Buck Henry, and one with I. A. L. Diamond. They're really great interviews. Nunnally Johnson says the whole thing in a screenplay is withholding information. A boring person tells you much more than you want to know at a party. Someone who just tells you everything is a bore, and you don't want to do that in a screenplay.

PIERSON: I think the mere fact that there are so many books out there and that we do think about things like three-act structure indicates that there's something there that needs to be thought about. Each one of us goes about dealing with structure in a different kind of way. It's like being an artist, a muralist. You're up there, and you're painting right here, but every so often you have to step back and see what you've just done to the total composition. Then you're in a position to come back and see what's gone wrong there. You can get back there, and that's when you become emotional. Now I step back and look at it with the other side of my brain.

KAZAN: The problem with these books is the tendency to want to spend a lot of time in the back of the room and not so much time up at the canvas. You have to be able to get lost in the canvas, and then when you wake up from getting lost, then you step back and see what you've done.

SWICORD: That's right. It's as if you are painting a mural, but you're standing in the back of the room and you're just looking at an unpainted wall. That's what they're saying in terms of putting the structure first. You have to have perspective, but there are two ideal times. One is before you start, when you're thinking about it. Don't spend too much time doing that, and then you write it. Afterwards you stand back, and that's the other time that you get perspective. You see what you've made, and you say, "Now I'm going to change it." Rewriting is the key for me—to not think I have to get it right the first time I write the scene.

PIERSON: Oh, God forbid. One of the terrible things about writing a screenplay is that for the first few weeks and months it's just awful. It's terrible to have to haul your ass to the computer every single day and confront this clear demonstration of your moral and intellectual bankruptcy. Each day you do something out of desperation with this shame and cold sweat pouring down your face so you won't have to step out into the world some day with something as bad as this. Then finally it begins to get good, and it's the rewriting that makes it good.

Caroline Thompson
on Structure

I am a writer. I love to write. I love words. Words are really important to me. Poetry of language is where I live. I think that a script is a reading experience first, and so our job is to make that reading experience vibrant and alive and challenging. Ironically, though, the greatest compliment you can get as a screenwriter is, "God, that was a quick and easy read," because it means you kept them riveted, you planted their ass in the chair, reading.

I don't write screen direction on a script because I think it throws the reader out of the story. I am very cunning, I hope, with how I construct the page, because I need the reader to focus on what I want them to focus on, and I need the director to follow my brain. Anything like an image that I really need them to pay attention to, I put them in capital letters on a single line, then I move along. I do not write big blocks of prose. My prose is not that long. I do not write dialogue that goes on and on . . . I understand that I am writing a sonnet, basically, and I discovered that I flourish inside those boundaries. To me, it is like writing a poem.

Getting lost in the detail is something I guess people do, but it is really important to be cogent and salient and relevant. The words are important. If you open a script and the opening line is, "It is a typical day on a typical street," nobody wants to read that, including yourself.

Lawrence Kasdan on the Rules
of Script Formatting

People used to say a movie script should be 120 pages. That's bullshit. They should be 100 pages long. No one will ever read it, and no one has ever given the note, "This script is too short." Never happened. It's a struggle to read a screenplay. I hate reading screenplays. I despise it, and I'm not alone. These agents, who are the first line of defense, and the producers, who are the second line, they hate reading scripts too, and they have piles of them.

Part of your job as an aspiring screenwriter—and that covers every screenwriter, because every screenwriter is trying to get over those fences whether he's established or not—is to get them through that script. If the first thing they do when they get the script is look at the last page and see what number's on it, then that's the most important thing. I'm the same way. If I get a script and I see 108, I say, "All right." If it says 120, I say, "Fuck." If you think it's really looking good at 140, you're kidding yourself.

I play a game where I just shorten the script by taking out sentences— "If I do this, I can lose two lines." That's a ridiculous game to play because what you're avoiding are the more important things. "Do I need this scene? Why am I taking so long to get through it? The first act is so long." That's always going to be the complaint. Every time someone reads your script, he's going to say, "You know, it took me a while to get into it," or, "It started a little slow." That's the nature of drama. In the first act, you don't know the people, you don't care that much, and you're setting everything up. If you've written a good screenplay, the second and third acts are going to be more interesting obviously and naturally.

It is true, however, that we all take too long setting things up. We put in way too much, and where it all comes out is when you make a movie, go into the editing room, and constantly ask yourself, "Why did I do that? I didn't need that. This actor looked at this actor, and I knew everything about the whole scene." At that point you kick yourself because you wasted a day or half a day, which you did not have and could not afford, doing something that was just as quickly conveyed by one look. You have to do that in the writing if you can. You may say, "I just finished another scene. It was a bitch, but I'm glad I wrote it. I'm going to tell my wife I wrote three pages today." What you really should do is take another breath and say, "Wait a minute. I didn't need these three pages, so really I wrote nothing today. But I learned from this. I didn't need that scene, and that's what I learned."

That is an enormously uplifting moment, actually. It fills you with energy, and you say, "It's working without that. I can get rid of that and still have the thing work." That's what happens in film editing, and that should be happening in the writing, assuming you don't mind writing the extra pages. Go ahead and write a 140-page script, but don't show it to anybody, because once you show it to them, you start to get defensive about it. They'll say they thought it was a little long or that you didn't need certain scenes, and you'll say, "Don't you see? You've got to have that scene. Otherwise, you won't understand." It's best to put it away for a week, and then come back and say, "140 pages? I wouldn't read this script. How can I get this down to 112 pages?"

I'll tell you a true story about *Raiders of the Lost Ark*. George, Steven, and I went off to a house, and we hashed out the story of *Raiders*. They said, "Go to it," and I didn't see them again for six months. I wrote the thing, and I think it was 130 pages. It seemed reasonable to me, and it was really good. So I took it to George, and he gave it to Steven. We all got together, and they said, "Larry, you've knocked it out of the park. It's great. We're going to make a deal based on this script."

Everything's cool, I'm very excited, and they said, "Now go back and take out 30 pages."

I said, "What? Thirty pages? This is really taut. It really moves like crazy."

They said, "We just want it to be about 100 pages, so take out 30 pages. You can take out this sequence or that sequence, but it's just too long."

I came back with 103 pages. I took out a lot of stuff I liked, and George's team looked at it and said, "This is great." The movie didn't get made for three more years, and during that time I did seven more drafts. George would add little things back, and Steven would add little things back. The script got a little bigger, then a little bigger, then a little bigger. I don't know what it wound up at, 120 pages or something, but it was at that 103-page length that it was the most muscular. It was the best version of it in a way. It was absolutely irresistible. You read it in like an hour. It taught me a big lesson, because I thought I was pretty self-disciplined, but I wasn't. To this day, it's a battle. Every time I do it, it's a battle to take out, take out, and take out. That should be another one of the many things you have on the wall in front of you—"Take out, take out."

> There was an old, very good writer of pulp novels who said, "In the first act, you get your guy up a tree. In the second act, you throw stones at him. In the third act, you get him out of the tree." That's the kind of thing I have to write down and look at every day. It's very helpful in constructing stories and can be applied to anything. ★ LAWRENCE KASDAN (*Body Heat, Raiders of the Lost Ark*)

Visual Storytelling

A Conversation with John August, John Lee Hancock,
and Randall Wallace

MODERATED BY BARBARA MORGAN

BARBARA MORGAN: Let's start off by having each of you, starting with John Lee, talk about the concept of writing without dialogue and how important that is in the process of your scripts.

JOHN LEE HANCOCK: I think usually when you come upon a story you're going to write, there are certain visual images you have in your head, and I think those are important to kind of have in your back pocket. There's something Clint Eastwood told me a long time ago that has been really helpful, not only in writing, but directing. He said when you shoot a scene, you ought to be able to pick one frame from that scene that tells the story of that scene. A picture. A photograph. And so when you think of that, it not only affects your blocking and things like that, but you think about the energy in a room or a conversation and the conflict and these kind of things. So I try to picture that when I'm writing a scene—What is the photograph of this scene that kind of tells a story? And that's from a photographic standpoint. That's it, just having images.

With *A Perfect World*, I started doing that *bass-ackwards*. Starting off, it was two different scripts I was kind of working on, and one of them started with the image of a little boy running around in a field in a Casper the Friendly Ghost outfit.

So I wanted to write a movie about that. Ideas come from the weirdest places. Obviously that's not enough for 120 pages, but it was thematically important for me.

JOHN AUGUST: Usually, in the process of writing, when it comes down to a scene level, I'm sort of looping it in my head. Basically I have an idea of what needs to happen in the scene, and I just sort of start running it in

                    RED
                 (yells)
          It's a deal.

                    BUTCH
                 (yells, OS)
          Make her say it.

Red looks to Gladys as if to say, "go ahead". She seems
reluctant. Red's frustration is showing.

                    GLADYS
          Phillip knows those things are
          against our beliefs.

                    RED
                 (to Gladys)
          What kinda' foolishness is....
                 (to Butch)
          She promises!

                    BUTCH
                 (yells O.S.)
          Make HER say it!

Red gives her a look that intones, "Say it or deal with me".

                    GLADYS
                 (reluctantly
                  yells)
          I promise.

EXT. CREEKSIDE - DAY

                    BUTCH
                 (to Phillip)
          Can we trust her?

Phillip shrugs his shoulders - "maybe yes, maybe no". Butch
reaches into his pocket, extracts the remaining wad of
stolen bills, unzips the Casper costume, stuffs them down
Phillip's costume, and rezips.

                    BUTCH
                 (to Phillip)
          When you get home, hide this.
          If she's lying you can buy your
          own damn beer. (beat) Now Buzz,
          listen here. I want you to
          step out there real slow, keep
          your paws in the air. Then
          strut right over to them cops
          and yell "trick or treat". Got
          it?

                         PHILLIP
                What are you gonna' do?

                         BUTCH
                . Somethin'll come to mind.

Butch sticks out his hand. Phillip shakes it.

                         BUTCH
                Bye Phillip. It's been one
                helluva' ride.

Butch gives the boy a gentle nudge toward the field.

                         BUTCH
                    (yells)
                All right, Cap'n. Make way for
                Casper the Friendly Ghost...
                the friendliest ghost I
                know...

EXT. ROADSIDE - DAY

Adler can't help but LAUGH as he watches through binoculars

                         RED
                Gimme' them things.

Adler hands over the binoculars. Red takes a look.

HIS POV

Phillip, nee Casper, walking in his full whitehood, arms
reaching for the sky.

EXT. FIELD - DAY

Phillip reaches level ground and sees the full strength of
the amassed police forces - at least 20 cars. Men with guns
everywhere - pointing toward him.

EXT. ROADSIDE - DAY

Red watches.

                         RED
                    (to himself)
                Come on. Keep walkin'. Why
                the hell is he stoppin'?
                    (to Gladys)
                Call for your boy to come.

a loop, and it gradually starts to fill out, and you start to hear the people talking to each other, and they keep talking and saying what they're going to say. And then you start to realize where they are and the space between them. Then you start to realize what's around them. And it sort of grows out of that.

I think the challenge for a screenwriter is always to put yourself in the audience. You as the writer have all this knowledge of who the characters are and what they are thinking and what they are doing. You probably know what that room smells like. But an audience member doesn't. All the audience gets is what you're putting in front of them and what they can hear. And if that isn't going to be enough to communicate what you need to communicate, you need to rethink how you're approaching the scene or whether this is really the right kind of story to be telling on a big screen. So it grows out of what the audience member would be experiencing sitting and watching that moment.

RANDALL WALLACE: It's such a great topic to consider, to think of visual storytelling as a unique category of storytelling. All storytelling has visuals as a part of it, but there are times when a picture could be something entirely different based on what you know about it or have just discovered about it. I had a mentor one time who said that the perfect screenplay would be one in which there was no dialogue at all. I don't really believe that, but it certainly is a challenge to figure out what—as John was saying about the Clint Eastwood bit of wisdom—would be the focus of a given moment.

There's a beautiful mural in the back of this room, and it reminds me of some of the great John Ford Westerns. David Lean would have a frame, and there would be just a tiny bit of character in it, a little bit of human life in it. And then a whole frame of people, the world around them. And that image itself evoked a sense of loneliness in size. But I started out just thinking strictly in terms of how you would tell a story to someone sitting around a campfire. I've come to this whole sense about what visuals are late, so I'm probably the least competent to answer the question, so I'll shut up.

AUGUST: I think there's an instinct that visual storytelling is about writing "angle on . . ." or the cut-tos or the helicopter shot of things. Very rarely in screenplays do you find yourself really needing to do that. As you're coming into a scene, it's painting just a few strokes, showing what the space is like and what the focus is going to be in those moments. It's grounding people enough so that they can have a sense of what this moment is and where this thing is, and it's building in those moments that are just going to be happening visually. Filmmaking is mostly about transitions, and so it's how you're going to get into that moment and how you're going to get out of that moment. And the first words you're throwing into a scene are what people are going to latch on to for the visual.

MORGAN: There's a film coming to mind that I think is a very high example of visual storytelling, and that's Bill Wittliff's *The Black Stallion*. It has a scene that, in my mind, goes on for twenty minutes, and there are no words spoken. It's between the horse and the little boy once they're stranded on the island. If you haven't seen it, it's a great film.

How do you go about creating something like that? What you get out of that scene is the boy and horse bonding so they become inseparable. How do you go about writing a scene like that, without the traditional method of dialogue, essentially painting a picture?

HANCOCK: I've got a situation on something I'm working on right now, and there are fifteen pages of a guy by himself, doing lots of different stuff, but with minimal dialogue. Maybe three pieces of dialogue in fifteen pages or so, and they're just like, "Hey," or whatever, things like that. So for me, it comes down to what John was saying about trying to give, in the fewest possible words, a very vivid idea or picture of what you're seeing.

I think we have to think of a screenplay not only as a finished product, a piece of art, and a blueprint for a film to come, but also as a sales tool. Part of your job in selling is to make sure that on the page your eyes are dancing not unlike they dance at 24 frames per second when we watch a movie. I think that's really important for the reader or the viewer to understand and get your point. You want eyes to dance on the page. The last thing you want is block text—blah, blah, blah. No one reads it. Think of it that way. Start from the standpoint of, "No one reads it," and then say, "Okay, how little can I get by with? How provocative can I make it? How can I give that example or metaphor or whatever lets people understand for themselves how potent this is visually and how packed it is from a dramatic standpoint?" I think when you do that, you go through and just clean it out. Rely on three- and four-word sentences, leave spaces, let people rest with the idea of provocative images and what you're trying to say.

AUGUST: I think that's one of the things that's changed about screenwriting over the last 50 years, 30 years—screenplays used to be a lot leaner. They used to be just, this is what happens, very much like a blueprint, like stick figures. As more and more people come into the process, and as the screenplay has this tremendous amount of responsibility on its shoulders before it becomes a movie, it's not just, "Hey, director, here's how to make this movie," it's, "Hey, Sony marketing team, this is what the movie's going to be." You have to create the experience of watching the movie just with the words on the page. Screenwriting's already an art of economy, but it's about being able to evoke a lot more with just a few small words.

I agree with what John Lee's saying in terms of precision and not giving people giant globs of text that are going to intimidate them. That's why you try to keep the scene description blocks less than three lines long if you can. You don't use full sentences if you don't have to. You try to give a sense of the visual pace of things with your sentences. It's not glamorous, and everyone thinks that screenwriting is the dialogue and the funny stuff, and so rarely is it that.

WALLACE: I have a couple of practical experiences with this that might be relevant. When we were doing *Secretariat*, there was a montage, and generally speaking, montages are like punting. It's like a default. We couldn't get a first down, so let's just kick it away. We can't find a way to tell this, so we'll just play a lot of music. We had a montage, and the montage was to tell the story of this magnificent racehorse who was winning all these races. Practically, this was going to be extremely time-consuming to shoot. Even though it might only be a third of a page, it was going to take hours and hours and setup after setup of horses running by just to shoot this thing.

My cinematographer is great, and he was talking about a piece of equipment called a phantom camera that shoots a thousand frames per second. I had no idea where we might use it, but he was just saying it's a really cool piece of equipment. So we had this montage, and I thought, "Instead of seven different examples of Secretariat crossing a finish line, let's just set up the camera and have one shot of the horse at a thousand frames per second running up and crossing the finish line." It became one of the most fascinating shots of the film for me. A single setup—we shot it in twenty minutes—but you see every articulation of the muscles of the horse, a galloping racehorse, and it becomes fascinating.

I think, on a certain level, surprise is the central currency of storytelling. What keeps the audience's eyes dancing? What keeps their minds sparkling as they're watching? It's revealing something new so that they don't want to turn away because they are being captured each time with that surprise.

If you have your audience—meaning your reader in the screenplay stage—gripped, then you can show them something that is strictly a visual image and might even take a sentence or two to describe and you won't lose them. I'll give you an example. In *Braveheart*, a moment that shocked pretty much everybody was when William Wallace is in the battle and pulls the helmet off of one of the guys attacking him and discovers the man is actually Robert the Bruce, the one he was trying so hard to get to be his ally. It is a wrenching moment for the audience. It's a surprise when people read it.

Shortly after that scene, there was another part of the screenplay, and the way it read was, "Robert the Bruce walked across the battlefield, red with the blood of his countrymen." And that's all it said.

But in that sentence was an image that was really haunting. A single image. I didn't describe what it would look like, but the emotional content of that bit in that place in the story implied to the cinematographer and the director and the actors and the set designer and everybody else what that had to be. I could see it in my own head, but I didn't know how to describe it in words other than emotional words.

In one of my first experiences in formal instruction in writing, the teacher showed us a short story. I think it was by Chekhov. In any case, I'm going to say it was because it makes me—with my accent—sound so much more sophisticated if I refer to Russian writers. He said the amateur will try, in order to describe a scene . . . The amateur will try to describe everything, but the professional will pick the single image that tells everything that needs to be said. Come to think of it, that echoes everything we're saying up here.

I think that even applies to dialogue. I bet a friend that the voiceover in *Braveheart* would remain in the final cut because he thought voiceover never stays. The opening voiceover in *Braveheart* is, "I will tell you of William Wallace. Historians from England will say I am a liar. But history is written by those who have hanged the heroes."

John is right, readers don't . . . When they see a block of dialogue, their eyes glaze over. I don't read blocks like that in my own screenplays. But dialogue is assertive. It's insistent, especially at the beginning. And if you can provoke the audience in any way . . . I think the Coen brothers had a movie, *Blood Simple*, that starts out with the character saying, "I understand over in Russia they got 'em a system where everybody looks out for everybody

181   VARIOUS SHOTS   181

The Scots, Irish and English are rained on by bolts, cutting
through their helmets and breastplates like paper.

MacGroom, Stewart and MacGregor are cut down.

Hamish and Campbell fight like Demons.

Longshanks and his entourage move towards the archers.

William runs through the Scots who are fighting like
Demons.

The English are being cut to pieces. Dead men and horses
are everywhere.

The Scottish infantry claws in, dragging down the horses,
hacking the knights as they run by.

182   AT THE ENGLISH COMMAND   182

Longshanks, Nobles and his generals ride in behind the
archers who are still firing.

                    LONGSHANKS
              Cease firing. Use the reinforcements!
              But bring me Wallace, alive if possible,
              dead is just as well. Send news of my
              victory later.

The General signals and the English reinforcements surge into
battle. Longshanks leaves.

183   IN THE THICK OF BATTLE   183

The arrows have stopped. William fights his way into the
watery edge of the field. William sees Longshanks and his
entourage leaving. He heads off on a horse for Longshanks.

One of Longshanks' Generals sees William and others
heading straight for them.

Still William fights on, meeting the charge. He hacks
down two riders. A third approaches. Although the horse
slams into William, he manages to unseat the rider.

The rider rolls to his feet. William struggles up to meet
him-- and comes face to face with Robert the Bruce.

(CONTINUED)

CONTINUED:

The shock and recognition stun William; in that moment
looking at Robert the Bruce's guilt-ridden face, he
understands everything: the betrayal, the hopelessness of
Scotland. As he stands there frozen, a bolt punches into the
muscle of his neck, and William doesn't react to it.

Bruce is horrified at the sight of William this way. He
batters at William's sword, as if its use would give him
absolution.

                    ROBERT
          Fight me! Fight me!

But William can only stagger back. Bruce's voice grows
ragged as he screams.

                    ROBERT
          FIGHT ME!

All around, the battle has decayed; the Scots are being
slaughtered. Another bolt glances off William's helmet; a
third rips into his thigh plate, making his legs collapse.
Suddenly Stephen comes through the melee, on Robert's horse!
He hits Robert from behind, knocking him down, and jumps to
the ground to try and lift William onto the horse!

Between William and the ARCHERS, a wave of fresh reserves
arrive.

Robert sees a knot of crossbowmen moving up, sighting out
William, taking careful aim! Bruce leaps up and helps
Stephen sling William onto the back of the horse, even covers
him with his shield, deflecting another arrow fired at
William, as Stephen mounts too.

As the horse plunges away into the smoke, Robert falls to the
water. His own troops reach him, realize who is, see the
horrible expression on his face, and race on after the Scots.
Robert is left alone, on his knees in the water, the fire and
noise of battle now dim to him, as if his senses have died
along with his heart.

184 EXT. ROAD - SUNSET   184

     Remnants of the defeated army straggle past. William and
     Stephen are trying to help Hamish carry his father, but now
     old Campbell says...

                    CAMPBELL
          Son... I want to die on the ground.

     But as they tilt old Campbell onto the ground, he grabs at
     something that starts to fall from the wound in his stomach.

                                              (CONTINUED)

184   CONTINUED: 184

                         CAMPBELL
               Whew. That'll clear your sinuses.
               Goodbye, boys.

                         HAMISH
               No. You're going to live.

                         CAMPBELL
               I don't think I can do without one of
               those...whatever it is...

          Hamish is too grief-stricken to speak.

                         WILLIAM
               You...were like my father...

          Old Campbell rallies one more time for this.

                         CAMPBELL
               ...And glad to die, like him... So you
               could be the men you are. All of ya.

          The last three words to Hamish, telling him he's a hero too.

                         CAMPBELL
               I'm a happy man.

          Hamish is weeping. When he looks up again, his father has
          died. We PULL BACK from them in tableaux, with the army, the
          people of Scotland, the whole gray world in defeat.

185   ROBERT THE BRUCE - DUSK   185

          walks through the battlefield, strewn with the bodies of the
          Scottish dead.

186   INT. EDINBURGH CASTLE - DAY   186

          William, still bloody and in his battered armor, removes the
          chain of office from beneath his breastplate, lays it onto
          the table in front of Craig and the other nobles, and walks
          from the room. Hamish and Stephen see the satisfaction on
          the nobles' face, and follow William out.

187   INT. CASTLE CORRIDOR - DAY   187

          Hamish and Stephen move out into the hallway after William--
          but he is gone.

188   EXT. WOODS - (GROVE)- NIGHT   188

          William is in the woods, in the grove of trees, looking at
          Murron's hidden grave.

                                                          (CONTINUED)

else. Well this here is Texas. And down here, you're on your own." When you hear that, I mean . . . I am with them. I am not going to miss another word of that story.

MORGAN: Each of you has written for other directors and also written and directed your own projects. Can you talk about how you protect your visual material? How you convey to another director what you intended? How does he or she get the point?

HANCOCK: I'm not sure you should do anything other than what you think is the best portrayal on the page. If they get it, you're in luck, and you have a good partnership. If they don't, I'm not sure there's anything you can add that's going to help them get it. Being a director has made me a much better writer. Since I've directed, my scripts are far sparer. It's a constant game of name that tune—I can name it in three notes—and cutting stuff out that's not necessary and coming up with something that's spare and waiting to be filled. I think that's the kind of stuff I react to when I read scripts to direct as well. They are not overwritten. I think that's almost a sin.

To be clear, I wasn't really talking about dialogue, in terms of block dialogue, although if you see a monologue that goes on and on without breaks forever, that's a sure sign of an amateur writer. Even if you do have a long, long monologue, you need to break it up. I was referring to text more than anything because I don't read it. I'll go, "Okay, he's describing the room. I get it. It's a pub. I've got one in my head. We'll find it on location scout." The more precise you can be and provocative . . . One line, and you're moving on.

AUGUST: I think early on, as you start to figure out the form of screenwriting and just how weird it is, there is this instinct to use descriptions like, "The room is 70 feet by 20 feet." You tend to be very literal about, "This is what you're going to see." And that doesn't help anybody. It doesn't give you what you need. Randall was saying, "What is the feeling of the place? What is the emotion of this?" Also, I've observed through my screenplays and other ones I've read, in those initial ten to fifteen pages, you're going to be doing a lot more setting up of the place and the world and the feel and the tone. And then you don't need as much of it as you go on because you get it.

Just like the setup of *Braveheart* is setting your expectations for what kind of movie this is, once those expectations are set, unless there's a reason why you have to reset those expectations, people are going to approach those things the same way. You don't need to keep talking about . . . If you're making *Marie Antoinette*, you don't have to keep talking about the dresses. We get that there are going to be pretty dresses. That's a big deal, but you don't have to keep hammering us on it. You can start focusing on other things.

In terms of directors, you're trying to give them . . . I write a lot of things for Tim Burton, and I'm just trying to find things I know are going to be interesting for him and that he's going to hit out of the park. I'll certainly think of images that would be suitable and appropriate for Tim to do, but I'm not . . . I hope it never feels like I'm telling him how to direct his movie. Directing from the page is when you start to feel like you're signaling every little dolly movement, and nobody wants that.

WALLACE: It certainly matters who the director is. You can only do so much about who you are, and you can only do so much about who they are. Mel Gibson directing *Braveheart* . . . Had it not been him, I think the movie would have been utterly different. With his own personal background and his own spiritual point of view, however that manifests, he understood, when he was reading the screenplay, that when William Wallace is praying the night before his execution, that was the Garden of Gethsemane. I wasn't thinking that when I wrote it, and he wasn't thinking that when he filmed it, but it was that thing of, "I know I am about to die, and now I am coming to terms with that." He had the same references that I had.

My next experience was with Michael Bay. It's really funny . . . It's been well publicized that Michael and I butted heads a lot. I found him really likable and charming. I really did. There were things about him that . . . I'm sure we wanted to throw each other through a wall. We had one discussion in which he came in and said, "Randall, what is all this Jane Austen fag shit?"

And I said, "Maybe you ought to be more specific."

He said, "This guy, he can't talk to a girl."

And I said, "All right, let's review the scene we're talking about. This pilot says to a nurse that he's just met, 'We're all being called away to battle. And every other pilot tonight is saying the same thing to every other nurse, "This may be the last night we're alive, so we better make it memorable." But I can't tell you that because I think I might be falling in love with you. And I know that to try to sleep with you would be wrong.'" This is all subtext, not text.

"'But I am going to survive. And when I come back, I'm going to find you, and we're going to have a chance to know if we're in love.' And he goes to the English Channel, and he's shot down, and he's in the freezing water for five hours. And then he's picked up, and he survives in the French Resistance. And he survives because he dreams that this woman loves him and he might know something he's never known in his life. And he comes back, and he has survived, and he wants to find her. And he goes all the way to Pearl Harbor, where she is a nurse. And he finds where she's working, and he sees her alone in the hospital during her last shift. And before he walks in, he thinks, 'What if what has kept me alive all this time is not real? How will I live then?' And he takes a moment to deal with it. Is that the 'Jane Austen fag shit' you're talking about?"

And Michael goes, "Yeah!"

And I said, "Well, that's because your idea of foreplay is 'See my Ferrari? Want to fuck?'"

And Michael said, "Yeah!"

So what happened was, he filmed some scenes that were verbatim what I had written and had exactly the opposite effect they were supposed to have. I cashed all the checks for *Pearl Harbor*. I sent my boys to college with it. But you always think, "What could it have been if it had been what I would have done?" What you end up with is, like in life, everything is a living dialogue. A good director brings—and Michael Bay is a great director—his own perspective. The interesting thing for a writer who directs is, we have that thing within our own heads. It's like that old song, "I may be schizophrenic, but I've always got each other." The director part of us is talking to the writer part of us, and when we're stuck in a scene, we can turn to our writer instantly and go, "Figure this out for me. Is it the words? Is it the scene?" And we try not to let the director beat up the writer too much in that process.

AUGUST: No script is director proof. You can't write a script that's so amazing that a director can't come in and make it do what you didn't want it to do. Even if you're directing yourself, you're going to change things. The writer-you is going to say, "What the fuck are you doing? That wasn't the point of this." But the director-you did the best he could and had different things happen on the day he was shooting the movie, and that's the reality and the challenge.

WALLACE: I once heard somebody who worked with Blake Edwards— Blake Edwards wrote, directed, and edited his own movies—he said that when Edwards was directing, he would cuss a blue streak about the idiot who wrote it like it was some other person. And when he was editing, he would cuss the director. Maybe that's a healthy approach.

MORGAN: How often do you, after your first or second draft, start going back through and removing much of what you've written to create more . . . ?

HANCOCK: I'm constantly doing that. When I reread stuff, it's with a red pen taking things out. I don't know about these guys, but some of the most fun for me is, after you've got a draft that's working, to sit there and start scrolling and reading and fixing. Then you start to look at it the way it appears on the page. You go, "This isn't aesthetically pleasing to me. I'm going to take this word out because I want this to be two lines instead of carrying over to a third. I'm going to change this adjective to a shorter one to get to two lines instead of three." Stupid stuff, but it's insanely fun.

AUGUST: It's a lot easier than actual writing.

WALLACE: Well, I had a funny experience. I come down here, and I think of John Lee because we—the way our lives are screwed up—both live in L.A. but see each other more here in Austin than we see each other in L.A. I once went to see John at his office at Warner Brothers, and he had a chart on the wall called "The Journey of the Hero." And I was looking at it, and I was thinking, "John has to use charts to write scripts." I'm looking at this chart, and I'm going, "Damn, that's exactly the way *Braveheart* unfolds. That's exactly right, that chart." I was just getting to know John then, and I was like, "So, how do you write your first drafts?"

And he goes, "Well, I usually like to write them in longhand first, and then I type them."

And I'm going, "Yeah, right. So behind the times." And now I'm writing that way. It's so much more organic. I don't feel that I have to lock myself in to what I'm doing. I'm playing first. I write it down, and then I go back and forth. I go between the computer and printing that out, but I always love having the pencil in my hand. I do believe that even if the process is stimulated by a block of dialogue that's too big or a desire to reduce the number of words, pressure oftentimes causes or prompts a much sharper exchange of dialogue. The less people say, the more you remember. The less the character says, the smarter he or she seems.

AUGUST: I think a good challenge for all aspiring writers is, practice by writing something that forces you to communicate a situation with more than one person in it, but that doesn't have people talking to each other. One of the things I'm writing right now is this movie called *Monster Apocalypse*, which is about giant monsters that smash buildings. It's really fun, but one of the challenges I set for myself is that there's not just one King

Kong, there are many, many King Kongs. You have a whole troop of apes who are lead characters in this story and should be able to carry . . . They have storytelling ability. As a screenwriter, it's a challenge to figure out the pack dynamic and what stories I can tell about the interpersonal conflicts between these apes who can't talk. And that's rewarding. It's a different kind of thing than we usually get to do, and it's like making a silent film, but with giant gorillas. That's why you sign up for this business.

MORGAN: Are you saying, essentially, to write a short story first by hand, or are you saying you actually write your scripts out in longhand?

AUGUST: I write scripts in longhand.

HANCOCK: I don't do it as much anymore, but back when I wrote *A Perfect World* I would write on the back of the script I had just finished—the one I was putting in the drawer because no one bought it—to save paper and kind of take a Spartan approach. It's funny, because at the Bob Bullock Texas State History Museum they had something about Texas movies a few years back, and they asked for things from movies filmed here. One of the things I had was the original script, written on the back of another one, with napkins stapled to it, ketchup stains from writing in the diner, coffee rings, all that. It's this massive bit of paper with all these different notes stuck on it and addendums and stuff, but I like that because it's real. It doesn't exist in the cyber world at all. It's this thing I can hold.

Then you reduce it to the computer. I'm old enough that I used to have to type the scripts. Sitting down to retype 120 pages was, for me, a two- or three-day ordeal. It's a huge time saver, and like I said, I love scrolling through and fidgeting and fixing stuff, but I do like to write the whole script longhand.

AUGUST: My basic process is, I sort of loop a scene, and when I figure out . . . When I see it, I'll do a scribble version, which is basically as quick as I can get it down on paper, so I don't forget. It doesn't look anything like the screenplay format. Then I'll write a longhand version of the scene with full dialogue and stuff like that. Longhand keeps me from editing too soon because I can't go back and keep rewriting the same scene. I think I write more sparely too because I have to move my pen around, and it's so much slower that I end up looking for exactly the right way to say something rather than typing three sentences when I could write one sentence. Then eventually I do type it.

WALLACE: I think the computer is a brilliant invention. It's fabulous to have, and there are times when I'll write my first draft just with a computer.

But I love the process of revising. It's funny, I loved walking through here on my way to breakfast this morning and seeing all these people sitting around with their computers, writing. It is so great to be around writers. But I think that ultimately you're writing your story inside your head, of course. And whatever the mechanical process is, there's always that moment, like when characters have a defining moment in a story.

Both of my grandfathers were dead before I was born. My father's father was dead before my father was born. My grandmother was a widow before she was a mother. And I desperately wanted to know who my grandfathers were. So I was eager to find those stories, and one day my father told me a single story about my grandfather. That story told me everything about who my grandfather was and who I was supposed to be. Everything. And in a way, I think that's what we do as storytellers.

If it takes 120 pages, and you think, "Well, if I don't have enough to make it a movie . . ." I mean the reason we're film writers instead of other kinds of writers is that we like the sense of fullness you can get out of that size format. Even if it's a two-hour story—and the story my father told me about my grandfather was about two minutes—there are going to be those moments in which characters stand up and define themselves. Sometimes they do it at the moment when they discover what's true about themselves. Any great story is going to have some of that—"This is where my line is. Cross this line, and I will fight you to the death." We're all looking for that, but sometimes the realization of what that is doesn't occur to us when we're in the formal act of writing.

I might be driving along in the car, thinking about anything but my story, and I'm listening to a song that's got nothing to do with the superficial text of the story I'm writing. All of a sudden I understand what has to happen, what he has to tell her, what she has to tell him, what they have to say to the world. And that is a process of working enough, with whatever tools you're using, so that the story is alive inside you.

HANCOCK: What Randy is saying is what I've tried to tell my wife forever and ever. I'm working even when I'm not working. Jack Nicholson says it more succinctly in *The Shining* when he's typing—"When you hear this noise, I'm working. When you don't hear this noise, I'm working."

MORGAN: How much does the concept of mythology help to convey a lot of these basic ideas you're talking about when you want to get them across without lots and lots of dialogue? Does it help?

HANCOCK: I think so. I think it would be foolish not to take advantage of mythology and stories that have held up through the ages. There's a reason why they are told and retold—it's because they work for us. Whether they are dramatic, romantic, or bittersweet, they tend to work, and that's why they are retold. I think you should be cognizant of that.

I'm never entirely rigid on, "Oh, this is the hero's journey." I approach it like a Chinese menu—I'll take a little of this and a little of this and some of this, and this seems a little like Joseph Campbell, and this kind of seems like, "Lord, lift this cup . . ." in the Garden of Gethsemane. They're good stories. Why not use that base?

AUGUST: More than mythology, I would say expectation. No matter what kind of movie you're making, there's a certain set of expectations that comes with it. If your movie is set in the Old West, people are going to come with their expectations of Westerns, so you don't have to explain what a rancher is. There's a shorthand you can use to fill in those things and expect that your audience knows enough to keep up so you can move ahead.

It's only if you're changing some things—the rules about how stuff works—that you need to be pretty explicit. If you're writing a vampire movie, but there are these three conditions, you let those conditions be known. You don't have to explain to them that the guy needs to drink blood because we know what a vampire movie is. And that's hugely helpful, but you'd be surprised how often you see these stories where, "I got that. I don't need to see that. I knew before I opened the script that that thing was going to happen."

The challenge of screenwriting is often getting rid of the curse of knowledge. As the screenwriter, you know why a scene is there. You know what's going to happen 30 pages from now. The person sitting in the theater doesn't know that. They're blank. Being a screenwriter is like continuously blanking yourself so that you're just the person sitting in the theater with only that information and recognizing what they have and what their next question is going to be. Anticipating that, honoring that, meeting their expectations most of the time so that they feel really smart, and then occasionally exceeding or defeating their expectations so they stay interested.

WALLACE: It's really fascinating, the question of mythology and our common understanding of stories from a culture. It really is true that the story isn't just told by the storyteller. The audience responds to the story, and the story becomes a part of a people. Maybe there is no single author of the King Arthur legends. The stories are told and retold and added to, and oftentimes we're drawing on mythology, but we only see it in retrospect.

I can give you an example from *Secretariat*, another one of those scenes in which we had such a limited budget to shoot and a limited schedule. There was another segment of montage about Secretariat training really hard for his final race. His trainers have chosen, instead of resting the horse before the longest of the Triple Crown races, to train him because the horse really loves to run. It's a dangerous and dramatic choice they make. So I was trying to think how to convey that. And again, I thought of a single scene. I hate to say it, but it was second unit. I wasn't even there. It's one of my favorite shots in the whole movie. The audience sees nothing but gray, and then slowly begins to understand there are waves in it. It's articulated. It's fog. And then there's a flash of lightning in the background, and Secretariat emerges from the fog with this primordial power. It's just a single shot, but it was like Pegasus running out of Mount Olympus.

You don't have to know about Pegasus and Greek mythology to appreciate that it's a powerful shot. Knowing that it's Pegasus may help or not help. What our myths are about are our deepest truths. They arise from our longings and our experience. And the closer we can get to those—that bedrock or that volcano—the sharper and more focused the single image can be, so that it sits us back in our chairs and makes us feel it.

Talking about images that resonate, I think another important thing is to leave some mystery. Mystery is powerful. An easy example would be a character who, at some point in the story, takes off his shirt, and you see on his back an endless array of scars. It's never explained, but you understand. It's like, "Oh, my father was in Vietnam," or something. He's never talked about it, and one day he sees him with his shirt off, and you go, "Oh, my God! What was that? Sometimes the mystery—just a slight visual image that alludes to it—will create a much bigger impression inside the audience than a whole bunch of . . . than knowing the actual story behind all those scars.

MORGAN: Is there a particular visual image that has resonated with you?

HANCOCK: Something I steal over and over again is Ethan outside the door in *The Searchers*, not really coming inside. Everything about that is just so . . . You get it. So I love images framed through doorways.

AUGUST: A much more recent example is the pilot of *Lost*, and there are many great images in it. We don't see the monster in *Lost*. We just see the tops of the trees moving. It seems like such a simple gag, but I was terrified of trees, far in the distance, moving. It just freaked me out. Good job, J. J. Abrams.

WALLACE: I really love *Doctor Zhivago*, and it was years and years later that I realized that, in part, I'd been living out, for twenty years, fantasies that had been planted in my head by watching that movie. There's a scene in which he's riding back home, and he's been to see his mistress. He loves her, but he loves his wife, and he's got to push on with his life. His horse comes to a stop, and then these partisans come and kidnap him or capture him. They ride across the road into the trees, and it all plays out right in front of us. And then the camera cranes up, and you see the endlessness of Siberia. And I thought, "What a perfectly powerful way . . ." I thought about that shot a number of times.

More than that is the scene in *Cool Hand Luke* when they're on the chain gang and this woman's washing a car. Her dress is wet, and she presses her knockers against the window of the car. I thought about that for years! Never could forget it.

5

Character & Dialogue

Building Characters and Mapping
Their Journeys

A Conversation with Lawrence Kasdan
and Anne Rapp

Making a Character Stand Out Immediately

ANNE RAPP: I don't consciously think that I want a character to burst out on a page. My characters, quite honestly—I don't think they do. I've been accused of writing movies that start out too slow, and it takes a long time to get . . . That's how life works. The writing process is almost like the viewing process in that when you get to know a character slowly and you're not so aware of so many things that have been thrown at you, they kind of . . . Then something happens—boom!

Thirty minutes into my first movie, an old lady shoots herself. All the stuff that happened in the first 30 minutes is crucial because of how everybody reacts. You understand the relationship of the loss, what people have lost by losing her. I think if you come out and hit that on the head in the beginning . . . I just kind of let them evolve in their own way. I don't know if that's the right way.

LAWRENCE KASDAN: I'm drawn to the same thing. All my movies start off very slowly, and I like that kind of movie. I like movies that start fast too, but I tend to prefer movies that start slowly. Invariably when people talk about one of my movies, they say, "It didn't really take off for half an hour until such and such happened." My reaction is always the same—it's defensive. I tell them I'm sick of how American movies have to move so quickly. It's the TV culture, where by the time you get to your first commercial, you have to have hooked the audience. The audience has to know who the good guys are and who the bad guys are. They have to understand the problem of the episode.

Carol Littleton is this wonderful editor who cut six or seven of my movies. She is a major influence on me. When she cut *Body Heat*, she was a little older than me but had done only a few movies. She left me after *Body Heat* and did *E.T.*, but then she came back to do *The Big Chill*. She's had an amazing career. When she says something, you have to take it seriously. So after I've held off all the philistines who want my work to play like a television episode, Carol Littleton weighs in, and invariably she says the same thing—the movie starts too slowly.

Movies really are different than novels or short stories or theater. In theater you can take your time. At the end of the first act, you can be an hour into the play, and it may be only then that you understand what the issues really are and what's really going on. You can define drama as taking a static situation and introducing an upsetting force. Literally, very often plays are like that. You can take as long as you want to establish the static situation. Perhaps it's a family, with its delicate balance of love and hate and jealousy and resentment. Then the prodigal son returns after traveling for ten years. Perhaps instead you have a small town that's held together by a balance of power, and then here comes a stranger, a music man with an instrument. It can be anything. Maybe you have guy who's been on the road selling things his whole life and suddenly loses his job. As his job is threatened, his whole sense of identity is threatened, and that affects his whole family. Movies don't work that way. The basic element of drama is the same, which is a static situation upset by something.

RAPP: I think it was Bill Wittliff who said, "Someone leaves home, and a stranger comes to town."

KASDAN: You can tell any story that way. In *Body Heat*, somebody comes to town. Matty Walker comes to Ned Racine's town. Sometimes somebody goes on a trip and arrives in a town.

RAPP: That's the stranger's story.

KASDAN: But movies do require a quicker start, and Carol Littleton's right. She always says, "You're doing too much padding. You're setting it up too much." But I do it because I'm drawn to all the quirky detail.

I say, "Don't you see how, when she's alone in her bedroom, she always puts her brush on her right-hand side? That's so great, isn't it?" But the audience is way ahead of you. Actresses like Glenn Close or Ellen Burstyn, they're geniuses at what they do. They've been to wardrobe, they've changed the way they walk and talk, and by the time they get to the make-up table, the audience already knows everything there is to know about the character. I don't care where the brush goes. It doesn't add any information, and that's really what movies are about. They're about using the most economical, muscular, and forward-moving approach possible.

RAPP: I read an interview with Horton Foote, who wrote character-driven movies and plays. He said he only started with a person and an event, and then just let that carry him. The important thing that I have to keep remembering is the event. I don't have any trouble starting with a person, but an event right off the bat really lets you off the hook, and that's the trouble I have. I can't get to that event quick enough. That's why I have to work hard. The other part, the characters, that's easy. They just evolve so much more naturally the way I write.

KASDAN: I think every one of us has strengths and weaknesses. Our weaknesses loom large for us. We've been struggling with them our whole lives. Our strengths we tend to discount and devalue. Characters are very easy for Anne. That is her natural bent. I think it's my natural bent. Plot scares the hell out of me. Story scares the hell out of me. Sometimes I've done good plotting and good story, but I never think so. I can always see the structure, the girders that are holding it up, and I think, "Can't everybody see that?" Whatever you worry about, that becomes very large. Whatever you're good at, that's very small.

RAPP: I'm about to adapt a book, and I've learned a big lesson on this. I sort of chose this book. It was given to me, but I chose to do it. The guy who wrote the book has the same strength I do. He also has the same weaknesses. I sort of naively said, "Oh, yeah, that's my territory. That's my kind of book. I can do that. It's a piece of cake." What the book needs, however, is somebody that can go in with much more drive and plot. I just add my atmosphere on top of his, and it just becomes this big mountain of atmosphere.

I think I was under the impression before this experience that strong plot really doesn't matter, that you can still compel the audience in the same way for two hours with your atmosphere, but that doesn't work. You need a combination of all of it. I purposely came into a panel right before this one with guys who were talking about heroes and villains. It was Shane Black and Scott Rosenberg, I believe. They like the totally opposite kind of movies that I like, and I thought, "I need to go listen to those guys because I have a hard time writing villains. Maybe they can talk about that."

KASDAN: What did they say?

RAPP: There's somebody who had a really interesting question, which I think was great. They kept talking about evil, but then someone just said,

"What is evil?" and all three of them just froze. They all write evil characters, so they started talking a little bit. What came out that I thought was really interesting was that we don't necessarily understand evil and don't have to understand it to write evil characters. If I had to say what the definition of evil is for me, it is the lack of compassion or lack of love. That's what evil is in the moment. That's just the kind of thing I think I need to explore, and it was really interesting to listen to those guys.

In a lot of movies, there's a tendency to have . . . There's no star. There's an ensemble of eight people of equal importance. That happens naturally with me. I don't mind that. I don't want to change the way I write. I don't want to change the kind of stories I tell. I like what I've written, and I like that *Cookie's Fortune* starts off really slowly. I like *Cookie's Fortune*, let me put it that way, but I do know that I need to work really hard at balancing my ability to write characters well with that other thing that I'm missing.

KASDAN: The only criterion in any kind of writing is, "Does it work?" The truth is, *Cookie's Fortune* doesn't start slow. It starts slow if you came to see *The Rock*, but the kind of people that are drawn to *Cookie's Fortune* didn't come for that. In fact, *Cookie's Fortune* works through that whole half hour because the characters are so interesting and funny and surprising. They may be very familiar to you, but they're pretty unfamiliar to me, and so I'm fascinated. It's like being on some new planet or something. It's not slow at all.

That same half hour's time, if it's not good or it's not new or it's not original, can be very slow. It can be endless. You can see an action movie where that's the case, and it'll seem like it's eight hours long. It's boring because you never cared for one second. What matters is, are the viewers engaged and interested? That's what makes it slow or fast.

The first rule of all filmmaking is that every scene should start at the last possible moment and end at the first possible moment. You want to come into the scene at the last possible moment where you can still understand what's going on. You want to come in so that the audience members have to catch up a little bit but are capable of catching up. You don't want them ahead of you. You don't want them waiting around, saying, "Get on with it. I get this."

Body Heat was the first movie I ever made. Carol Littleton and I were sitting there. I had done one of these writing things where you do something twice. I do it all the time. You like it so much, you do it twice. You think, "I can't make that jump so fast, so I'm going to do it in stages." So I had another attempt on the husband's life that didn't work out. There was a screw-up. They had to call it off at the last minute. They were going to kill him, and he had a gun. She signals him to fade away, and he does fade away. So now he's come so close to this that he's lost his nerve, because he doesn't have that much nerve to begin with.

There's a scene, one of the better scenes in the movie, where she comes into his apartment and slowly, slowly takes off her clothes. She doesn't do it in a sexy way but in the way she would if they had been husband and wife for ten years. She's just getting ready for bed. What she's really doing is, she's slowly reeling him back in, because she knows exactly what's happened, which is that he's lost his nerve. That scene was really good. By the end of it, he's ready to give it another shot, and then he goes out and kills the husband.

It took Carol a long time to convince me that we didn't need that because the audience was so far ahead of us. To do it twice was really testing their patience. So we just lifted that out, which was really hard for me. It was my first movie and a scene I really liked in the middle of it. In fact, we had to use the beginning of that scene to get him out of the bed and into the real scene. You don't notice this, but there are really clear shots of the bed, and the sheets change. It's two different nights. No one notices, of course. That was another big lesson for me, that no one is paying attention to anything.

Individual Voices in an Ensemble Piece

RAPP: If I have two characters that sound too much alike, I figure I don't need one of them. I'm always looking for somebody to cut out, because I always end up with too many characters. That's something to consider.

KASDAN: The problem is recognizing when they sound too much alike. In my head they all sound different. I've already sort of cast them with fake actors in my head, and they sound completely different. Their tone and their jokes are different. I think that's the essence of this panel—how do you make a personal, believable person? It doesn't matter whether it's an ensemble piece or there are three people in the whole movie.

The genius of the '40s screwball comedies—and this is what I've tried to do in every movie I've ever written, whether it's a comedy or a drama—is that in two or three lines they were able to give personalities to secondary characters. Hollywood lost any interest in doing that for 30 years because they were really only interested in the movie star and his girlfriend, and the movie star and the other movie star. Scripts are driven by studio executives who understand nothing but the books on screenwriting they've read, and so they don't understand that it matters what the gas station attendant says, even if he only has two lines. Those two lines really affect the feel of the whole movie, your sense of the richness of it, the reality of it, and what kind of value you assign to everything that happens in it.

When you treat people as though they're ciphers it devalues the whole movie. The challenge of real character writing is in establishing, in the shortest possible way, a clear sense of the individuality of a person. It's a rigorous, rigorous problem. You can't just say they pulled in, got gas, and left. The attendant said, "Can I help you?" Then he said, "Thank you, sir." It would be better to just cut to them pulling out of the gas station. We don't have to see them there unless there's a reason, and maybe the only reason is the attendant. What do the people in this area think of a car like that? Is there something about the way this couple looks that's suspicious? You can have a perfectly normal couple from Los Angeles pull into a gas station in Lubbock, and they're going to look like Martians, so you better have that gas station attendant, even if he doesn't say anything, look at them like they're Martians. And he better deal with them—the way he takes their money or credit card or anything—as though they're Martians.

Look at any Preston Sturges movie. Preston Sturges actually writes long raps for people who will never come back into the movie just because he likes the sound of it. Look at any Capra movie. Look at Howard Hawks's comedies and John Ford's Westerns. John Ford had wonderful writers working for him. In *My Darling Clementine*, Wyatt Earp walks up to the bartender and says, "You ever been in love?"

The bartender says, "No, I've been a bartender all my life." That's it. That's how long it takes, but you've got to be a great screenwriter.

RAPP: Those things come to you when you least expect them. If you have too much of a game plan—you know exactly who these characters are in this movie before you ever start writing—you've already fooled yourself, because in my experience, one of your main characters is not even planned when you start writing the script. Someone pops out. Someone just forces his or her way in.

What happened in *Cookie's Fortune* was, the young girl played by Liv Tyler was never part of the game plan. She was never something Altman and I discussed. She was never in my short story that I had started to write. Twenty pages into the first act she just appeared, and I went with it because I kind of needed her voice. By the end of the movie, I think the movie's point of view is her point of view. She's probably the second most important character. "Important" is not a good word, but . . . She wasn't even planned. It's like you don't have to know too much when you start these things. A lot of times that stuff will happen.

KASDAN: Screenwriting is different from all other kinds of writing. You don't have as much freedom. A short story can be almost anything. A short story can be eight pages about sitting down in this chair. You could never do that in a movie. Actually, you could do it in a movie, but it would be a short film and be shown at a festival. Regular movies are all about economy, economy, economy. How do you condense, condense, condense?

Very often the character that jumps into the movie and won't shut up is the one that's speaking for you. You have all these feelings about these characters, but you don't really have a voice, and sometimes you want a voice. Sometimes you want to say, "You know why I think these people are wonderful or funny?" You want something that makes it possible to express your feelings, and this other character does that. Liv does that in your movie.

RAPP: People in Hollywood like to ask you all the time—and it's an important question, I suppose—"What's this movie about?" It's hard for me to say what my movies are about in a sentence. I wish I was one of those writers who can say, "It's about a six-year-old that sees dead people," and that describes the whole movie.

When that character jumped out—and Liv Tyler did it beautifully, I thought—it sort of occurred to me that the movie is about family pride and how it can be such a great thing and such a horrible thing. It's about family pride, and she represented that to me. I didn't realize it when I was writing it, but she hated everything about the town. She hated everything about her family. She kept running off, but she kept coming home. Charles S. Dutton's character, that's the best family she could have, and he is her family. But those things sometimes aren't planned. That's a scary way to write. You don't have a game plan.

KASDAN: I didn't really finish my thought. Screenwriting is this highly compressed, very economical form of writing, but you can't take the air out. You can't take the unknown part or the part that surprises you out of it. Maybe some character starts talking to you, and you wish he wouldn't because now it's taken a page and a half, and you need that page and a half for the principal, but you must leave the air in. Otherwise you will end up with a dead screenplay, which is mostly what we see in the theaters.

The ones you want to write are never like that. They're the ones where every page contains a surprise. Even within this extremely disciplined, ritualized form, you have to leave that surprise. If you didn't know every day there was going to be a surprise, how could you ever get to the desk? It would be so fucking boring.

RAPP: Those guys in the other panel, they say "fuck" all the time, so it's okay.

KASDAN: Well, okay then.

Nicholas Kazan on
Writing Characters

One thing I always try to do is look at every character. Thank God for computers, because you can just put a search in. Put in your main character, put a search in, and just look through all the dialogue of that character. See if the character has a verbal tic in one place. He called somebody "buddy" once. That's kind of nice, so maybe he should call everybody buddy. Then you look through, and there are a few more places to put it, and suddenly the character starts to have a little bit more texture.

You have a character who's formal, who doesn't use contractions. You notice that in one place, and it feels good. You think maybe the character shouldn't use contractions ever. Then you go back and search for this character named Norm, and Norm always speaks in very formal speech, and then Norm takes on more life. Go back and look at all of those.

The Protagonist

The protagonist has to drive the story. The protagonist can't be passive. We all have a tendency—because so many things happen to us in life that aren't in our control—to have things just happen to our protagonist. That doesn't mean you can't have something happen to him at the beginning. Something happening to him at the beginning is good. His father dies, his girlfriend leaves him, his house burns down, and then he has to start over. Those are sort of the inciting incidents that get the movie started. All those things happen, and the question is, how does this person put his life back together? Once the person starts to put his life back together, everything he does can't be determined by other people. It has to be determined by him.

If you have a section that doesn't seem to be working, you say, "Something's wrong here. It doesn't seem as interesting." It's quite possible that for a little while your protagonist is being passive. He's not driving the story. Always take a look at it.

There are tricks to be used here. Even the illusion of activity is better than no activity. Let's say halfway through the story you need to have the boss get fired and a new boss come in who's horrible. What you want to do is have the boss's firing be somehow related to the actions of the protagonist. For instance, your protagonist could do something good. He could do a good job, which somehow backfires and gets his boss in trouble, and then the boss gets fired, but then this new boss is a pain in the ass as a result of the protagonist's actions. It doesn't have to be a big thing either, just a little thing that starts the ball rolling so everything builds on everything else.

The Importance of Characters' Names

Changing their names is actually very good. There are times . . . I have a screenplay I just turned in last fall, and I changed the main character's name three times because it started out based on a true story. I began with a real person's name, and then I realized the real person was too boring, so I reconceived the character and changed her name. Then I realized, although that was interesting, I had to go a different way. I changed the name again.

When you have to reconceive a character, you should always change the name. Sometimes you keep some of the dialogue. That's fine, because different people can say the same things. Everybody can say the word "no." Everybody can say more elaborate things too. You have to be very careful that you're not using an old voice.

Crafting Characters

A Conversation with Lawrence Kasdan

Part of the writing job is to be very perceptive about people and how odd people are and how unpredictable they are, but you have to use what Malcolm Gladwell calls "thin slicing." You get an impression of someone, and you can get a sense of his or her whole being from that one impression, so your very brief contact with someone may suggest a whole character. That happens to you in real life, and sometimes you're right and sometimes you're wrong about who the person really is. But in writing, that's your whole job, because in a movie, which is so economical, all you're ever going to have of a character is a thin slice. Maybe he has four minutes of screen time, but that's a big part in a movie.

Most American movies are centered on one protagonist, maybe two if we're lucky, and so they get an hour and a half on screen. But all the interesting characters, the secondary characters, they have to be established in tiny amounts of time, so you want to put them in a situation where they can reveal who they are. What do they care about? What are they afraid of? You want to add to those characters, and the major characters, all the quirks and specific details you can possibly come up with so the audience doesn't feel, "I've seen that. Show me something new."

As an example, in *Body Heat* you see that William Hurt's a runner. He cares about his body. He runs first thing in the morning. He runs along the beach, on the boardwalk, on the pier, and then he stops, pulls out a pack of cigarettes and starts smoking. You know a lot about him from that, and that turns out to be important in the movie. He has a certain kind of discipline and yet no discipline. He wants to keep fully in shape and sexually ready to go, but he's ready to let his core turn to rot. He's susceptible to addictions, which is what the movie turns out to be about. He becomes addicted to a woman. It's just a tiny little thing, but you see what his character is like.

Another big moment in the movie is when someone says, "Do you mind if I smoke?" and everyone else is relieved, and the whole room fills with smoke. Ted Danson is just sort of watching them. He is the one pure character in the room, because everyone else is completely compromised and corrupted in some way. Someone offers him a cigarette, and he says, "No, that's all right. I'll just breathe the air." That line really speaks to the whole story, because he is moving in a world that is completely corrupt. He is breathing the air all the time. You can have the highest intentions, but if you swim in dirty water, you're going to catch some of the dirt, and that's what happens to the Ted Danson character. So that's a little bit of character building.

On the Influence of Akira Kurosawa

Akira Kurosawa is the best teacher in the world, and not just in terms of directing, although I think he's the best director in the world, the best with actors, and the best with placement of the camera. He revolutionized the way we cover action and drama. He did every kind of film. He worked in every genre. He was like Shakespeare, except in film. There's no one equal to him. He made these tiny, intimate human dramas like *Ikiru*. He made the best action movie ever made with *Seven Samurai*. If you haven't seen these movies, you must see them. You have to go out and get those movies immediately.

The most entertaining movie ever made is *Yojimbo*, and it's been ripped off several times. It was inspired by a Dashiell Hammett novel called *Red Harvest*, which is worth reading. It's about a guy who comes to a town where everybody in the whole town is corrupt. He assesses the situation for a while, figures out how he can set one bad guy against another, and essentially cleans up the entire town by having them destroy each other. That's what happens when Sergio Leone ripped it off, and it became *Fistful of Dollars*. It's been done many, many times. Walter Hill, who's a friend of mine, did it again as *Last Man Standing*.

If you want a lesson in character building or writing, you could watch any Kurosawa movie, but you should start with *Seven Samurai*. I think you all know the story of a town under siege by bandits. They have no money,

11. EXT. THE BEACHFRONT - NIGHT   11.

     Racine comes out of the structure. And stops. Matty is
     gone. Racine looks around without much hope. Finally,
     he puts a wet paper towel to the back of his neck.
     We begin to hear a strange, measured THUMPING, and then...

12. EXT. THE BOARDWALK (82ND ST.) - DAWN   12.

     Racine is running. The THUMPING is the sound of Racine's
     battered running shoes hitting the weathered wooden planks
     of the Boardwalk. Racine wears old gym shorts and a torn
     tee-shirt with "F.S.U." fading from the front. The raised
     wooden walk works its crooked way through lush, tropical
     vegetation, first coming close to the wide, white beach,
     then jutting back inland, swallowed by greenery, then
     shooting out again toward the sea. Racine hits this last
     stretch at top speed and launches himself flying out onto
     the gleaming sand.

13. EXT. BEACH - DAWN   13.

     Racine is running on the sand now, on a raised, hardened
     section that bisects the beach. His shoes make a weird
     WHOOSHING sound each time they break the compacted
     surface and sink an inch below. The sun is just rising
     from the ocean to his right, yet the day is already broiling.
     Racine's shirt is drenched. The WHOOSHING is hypnotic,
     steady; his expression indicates that it is just this sound
     which keeps him going.

13A EXT. THE BAND SHELL/THE BEACH - DAY   13A.

     Further on, Racine runs by the Band Shell where he'd
     seen Matty.

14. EXT. THE PIER - DAY   14.

     The THUMPING returns, as Racine runs the long, straight
     pier directly out to sea, toward the rising sun. A
     Lifeguard Boat with an outboard motor is on the left of
     the pier. Racine watches it as he runs until it disappears
     beneath him, then reappears on his right and turns out to
     sea, so that it is running beside him. Racine speeds up,
     really kicking, racing the boat to the end of the pier.
     The Lifeguard on board isn't even aware of Racine, but
     he beats the runner nonetheless, then veers off to continue
     his business.

     Racine pulls up, breathing hard. He walks it off a bit,
     watching the boat, then turns and starts walking back
     along the pier. He reaches into the waistband of his
     shorts and takes out a pack of cigarettes.

15. INT. RACINE'S OFFICE - DAY   15.

     Racine is behind the desk. Occupying the two seats in

                                        CONTINUED:

so they send a couple of their people to a border town to find some samurai to protect the town against the bandits. So these guys who have no money and nothing to offer give rice to the samurai although they're eating millet themselves. The samurai don't understand that at first. The villagers have to find samurai to protect them, and samurai who would do it for nothing.

They have to find one guy to galvanize the group, and that leader in the American version, *The Magnificent Seven*, is Yul Brynner. But the Japanese actor who plays that role is spectacular, and he's so charismatic and full of integrity and honor that he's able to convince five more samurai to join him, so that's six. Then they have the one guy, Toshiro Mifune, the greatest Japanese action actor of all time, who's rebellious and wild and joins them sort of against his will. So there are now seven samurai, and they go back to this little town.

In gathering this group, which is also the model for *The Dirty Dozen* and every movie like that where a team is put together for specific skills, you see some wonderful character writing as the leader who's collecting the group scans the town to find likely samurai. He can tell just by looking at some samurai that they'll only do it for the money. He can see that others have a strain of integrity and compassion in them, and they're possibilities. So then he'll send the villagers to try to get the samurai to come in and have an interview. The way each one of them approaches the door to come into the shack where he's interviewing people tells you everything about the samurai's character, his fighting style, how smart he is, and how cautious. Some walk in, get hit on their heads, and they're mad. Others come to the door and stop—"No tricks, please." They know that's the kind of samurai he's looking for, someone who can sense where the danger is. He meets old friends. He meets people who have survived battles. They talk a lot in this extended section where he's gathering the team about life and death and doing things for reasons other than money.

By the time the group sets off for the little village, you're in love with all seven samurai. You feel you've touched upon every major theme in human drama. It's about life, death, compassion, generosity, fear, and overcoming your fears. It's spectacular. And talk about classic character introduction— a bandit that got interrupted in his crime has taken a child into a barn. You see this guy who will turn out to be the main samurai at the river shaving off his samurai ponytail. He does it very calmly. You see the way he moves and the kind of peace he has. He is making himself up to look like a monk.

He goes to the barn and speaks to the bandit. The bandit's terrified and therefore dangerous, and the child is in jeopardy. You never see the bandit. You just see the older samurai talking to him. He's offering him balls of rice. Then there's a moment, one of the greatest action moments in history, where the samurai hands the bandit the rice ball and then pauses for a second. Suddenly he moves from slow to very fast. He goes in, things slow down, and the bandit comes out. He's been killed. He's holding his stomach and falls flat on his face. Then the older samurai comes out with the child.

So you've seen this incredible man of action pretend to be a man of peace, a monk. There's a kind of serenity about him and yet enormous skill, competence, danger, and everything we find romantic and attractive about these kinds of characters. It sets the tone for the entire movie. It's the first thing the villagers witness in the border town, and it shows them that this is the guy who's going to be able to help them. Of course he resists at first, but his heart is too big. If you just study that movie and watch it once, your mind will be blown. Watch it twice and you'll say, "Oh, my God. There's storytelling revealed here that I've never understood."

The Empire Strikes Back and the Journey of Self-Discovery

Through various circumstances I had the opportunity to write *Raiders of the Lost Ark*. It was my first job, and I worked on it for six months. It was very hard, and I was very proud of what I'd done. I flew up to where George lived and gave it to him. I walked into his office and said, "Oh, hi." He took the script, threw it on his desk, and said, "Let's go to lunch." We went to lunch, we sat down, and after a while he said, "How would you like to write *The Empire Strikes Back*?"

I said, "What?" because I knew nothing about the project, other than that a great old-time screenwriter, Leigh Brackett, was working on it.

He said, "Leigh Brackett turned in a draft, but it was not what I wanted. Very sadly, she's died, and we're already building sets in England. I need a script."

I said, "Don't you want to read *Raiders of the Lost Ark* before you offer me this job?"

He said, "I'm going to read it tonight, and if I don't like it, I'm going to call you tomorrow and take back this offer." But he did like it, and so the next day I was working on *Empire Strikes Back*.

I went back a week later, and we sat down and started talking. Irvin Kershner, the director, was there. He'd made a couple of adventure films, including *The Return of a Man Called Horse*, but he had never done anything like *Star Wars* or *Empire Strikes Back*. He had been a teacher of George's at USC, and George was very aware of his immense talent, so he hired him for what was the greatest job available, which was to do the sequel to *Star Wars*. The three of us came into George's office, and George said to me, "Darth Vader is Luke's father."

I said, "No shit!" That was the coolest thing I had ever heard, because it was clear George was going to take what was already the biggest hit in history and make it much more interesting. He was going to follow through on some things that were suggested in the first movie that would make the sequel even better in some ways. He was going to get into family issues, including the relationship between parents and children, which is basically what all stories are about. We spend our whole lives trying to figure out those issues, and we react both consciously and unconsciously to things our parents did to us and the examples they gave us in their own lives. It's a burden we carry with us our entire lives, and it's one of the major themes in any kind of writing. It doesn't have to be about your literal father. It may be your mentor, the one who showed you the way your life should go, or the one who stopped you and said, "No, you can't do that." Did you let that person rule the day or not?

I always say there are three stories. In the first, someone comes to town. That's *Seven Samurai*. In the second, someone goes on a journey. That's what most movies are about. In the third, someone goes on a journey *and* comes to town, but the journey can take many different forms. You can go on a journey and never leave your hometown. You can go on a journey, and because of something your father told you, your find out your whole life is wrong.

The unreliable narrator is a wonderful conceit that comes up very often in really good novels. It's very easy to mislead the reader of a novel. You can have a novel going for 200 pages, the main character is narrating it, and you think, "I think I get this story." Then something happens, and you realize the entire story has been warped by the narrator's prejudices or fears or myopia, or perhaps he's working out some grudge, and nothing you've read so far can be taken seriously. That can happen to you in life, when you realize that someone who is very important to you is an unreliable narrator. Perhaps you're very young when you first hear a story, and you accept it, and then years later you have a moment of epiphany and say, "Holy shit! They were wrong about everything." Then you have to think back on every decision you've made up until that point that was based on that information.

Sometimes the unreliable narrator, the one giving you the bad information, is you. That's a pretty good story in itself, when you have to reevaluate everything you've done. For some of us, that happens every morning. You think, "I'm doing something wrong. I got off on the wrong foot here somewhere. I've got to trace my steps backward and try to figure out why I'm here now instead of doing the things I want to do." I think all of us feel that way at some point during the day, the week, the month, or the year. You'll say, "Is it possible to go back and rectify my mistakes?" There's a very good story in the unreliable narrator or the unreliable mentor.

The story "someone leaves town" or "someone goes on a journey" could be that the character goes on a journey from all his previous beliefs. That's tough to do in a movie, but it can be done. He is going on a journey of self-discovery and liberation that he didn't expect. With *Empire Strikes Back*, Lucas was going to take the story back to Oedipus. Darth Vader was the bad father that had to be destroyed in order for the son to be released.

What's very common is "someone comes to town." That's basic drama. You'll have a dramatic situation, whether it's that bad guys come to town, or a marriage has been going on for 25 years, or a high school kid is being ostracized by a group. It's just a situation. Then somebody comes to town, whether it's the new kid at school or the lover that enters a marriage, and that character shakes up everything. In *Red Harvest* it's a very complicated, dangerous guy who comes into a corrupt situation and smashes it all into little pieces.

I think the reason a lot of people like *Empire* the most and *Jedi*, which I also wrote, strikes them as kind of a disappointment is that *Empire* is the second act of a three-act play. The way classic drama works is that the first act sets up the situation. You see the dilemma. In the second act, the complications ensue, and by the end of the second act, if you've been successful, it appears that the dilemma cannot be resolved. Our hero will never get out of this, and the people we care about will never be able to solve this dilemma. Then, in the third act, you solve it.

When Your Characters Surprise You

It's always a good thing, assuming it's going in the direction you wanted to go when you started out, but often the direction we wanted to go when we started out is wrong. Writing is like taking a drug or getting drunk. It's like any loss of control. You're going to go places you don't expect. You may wake up somewhere, and you don't remember how you got there. What you hope is that you've set the ground rules for the thing in such a way that you're still in the ballpark. You may be way out in the bleachers when you expected to be at first base, but you're still in the ballpark.

Sometimes you wake up after writing for six weeks, and you look at it and say, "I lost the ballpark. I'm not even in the right neighborhood." That's disheartening, but you have to remain calm like you would if you were lost in the city and say, "What do I recognize around here? Maybe this neighborhood is just as good a neighborhood for me as the one I intended to be in." Be open to the possibilities. That's not a bad plan for your whole life. When you meet someone, be open to the possibility of that person, even if he or she initially puts you off. Be open to the possibilities of story. Be open to saying, "This is not what I thought I was doing, but this is what I *am* doing." Be aware of the change and try to know when it's worth pursuing and when it isn't, or when you're just lost and have to throw out some of your work. Before you start throwing anything out, be open to the idea that you've arrived somewhere for a purpose.

It's like stumbling through the woods. You never know what's coming, what's behind the next bush or around the next curve. My wife and I have a place in Colorado, and the most fun is walking in the mountains and along the trails. They take you right back. You could be in a fairy tale. You could meet a giant, a troll, a fairy, a witch, anything on those trails. Those stories have proved themselves for thousands of years because the woods are a very powerful metaphor. If there isn't a powerful metaphor working for you in your story, you're probably on the wrong track. Innocence or evil or anyone stumbling through the forest is a very powerful metaphor for the unexpectedness of life, the dangers, and the possibility of discovery at the return. It's very powerful.

Recently I was at this amazing concert, and one of the people there was Werner Herzog. There was a brief interview with him in which he was talking about a movie he made called *Fitzcarraldo*. The story in *Fitzcarraldo* is that this mad German guy wants to build an opera house in the jungle in South America, and in order to fund the building of the opera house, he gets into the rubber business. He needs to reach this really profitable parcel of rubber trees, so he eventually has to haul the gigantic steamship he's using to sail down the river over the mountains. They actually did that when they were making the film. They didn't use any tricks or anything, and only an obsessed, half-crazed director like Herzog could have done it. It's a very powerful movie, and in some ways the making of it is more powerful, but what he said that so struck me was, "I knew that hauling the steamship over the mountains was a powerful metaphor, but I didn't know what it was a metaphor for." That's sometimes what making art is about, stumbling ahead into the darkness and hoping that whatever got you going will get you there.

Thoughts on Character

It's as if you were painting a painting and said, "I don't want just one color. I want several colors. I know this yellow looks good next to this blue, and this blue looks surprising next to this orange." That's exactly what you're doing when you're writing characters. You may say, "These two characters are subdued in a way that serves my story but does not serve the excitement and drama of the movie. I need to bring in somebody who will wake the thing up and draw out my characters so that they reveal more of themselves." This other character may allow them to be revealed because he challenges them, he threatens them, he's reckless in a way that they aren't, and he's funny in a way that they aren't. Suddenly you've enhanced some of your characters through this other character.

Balancing a Large Ensemble

It's tough. It's not a popular genre in Hollywood. Now, there are things that look like ensemble movies that are these horrible movies where you get 25 movie stars to each work for a week, and it's about Halloween. They look like ensemble pieces, but they're not ensemble pieces. Real ensemble pieces are hard to get made, and that's pretty much the only kind of movie I've made.

My first movie was *Body Heat*, and it had William Hurt, Kathleen Turner, and two other characters, really—Ted Danson and J. A. Preston, who played the cop. Most of the movie was just Bill Hurt and Kathleen Turner, and so it was the three of us making this movie, and it was a very intense and claustrophobic story. All I had ever wanted to do was make movies, but when it was over, I was worn out with how small and tight it was. Even though I loved making it, every day there were the same three personalities, and I said, "I'm going to write a movie with seven or eight leads in it because I like actors, and I don't want to be stuck with just two actors." That's how *The Big Chill* came about.

I wanted to tell that story, and I brought in a friend of mine to write it with me. We managed to get seven leads, essentially, and I loved it. I absolutely loved it, because I love actors, and I love the way actors are with each other. With so many leads, there are lots of combinations going on there, and the possibilities for scenes are endless. I was very taken with it. I've directed eleven movies, and I'd say eight of them are ensemble movies.

A movie like *The Big Chill*, the studios all turned it down. They said, "You can't have seven protagonists. We don't do that. You don't know who to invest in. You don't know who the story is about."

I said, "What? I don't understand what you're saying. This can work. This is a group of people, and you'll get invested in all of them. It'll be fun."

The first time we screened it, the studio head came out and said, "I had no idea this was a comedy." That was very satisfying. There's nothing more satisfying than you having an idea, they say it won't work, and it does work. Usually it goes the other way. They say it won't work, and it doesn't work.

The one I just did is sort of an ensemble movie with Diane Keaton, Kevin Kline, Richard Jenkins, Dianne Wiest, Elisabeth Moss, and Mark Duplass. Each day you get to work with a lot of people who are all funny, good, and smart. It's just like putting together an all-star team. You get ten great actors for every part, you get to work with the best people, and you feel like the manager of a team. I'm very drawn to it.

Still, the manager of the team has the responsibility to put the best players in each position, and as a writer, that's what you're doing too. You're creating the most interesting person to play shortstop, third base, and center field. If the infield is a certain kind of way, you want the outfield to be different. You want to mix it up, match it, and have it help you tell the story. You can make the center fielder a troublemaker, the catcher reliable, the first baseman vain, and the third baseman industrious and honest. Suddenly you've got a team.

Dialogue and Finding the Voice

A Conversation with John August and
John Lee Hancock

JOHN AUGUST: If you're looking through a script and there's a line of dialogue that any character in the script could say, there's a problem—unless you're writing a *CSI* episode, where people have to talk about the evidence. In a movie there should be only one character that can say a given line or convey a certain message. Hearing those voices is really just thinking through all the people you encountered in your life and how their voices are different and closing your eyes and listening to the patterns of how people speak and finding a way to reflect that on a page.

JOHN LEE HANCOCK: I just did a rewrite on something and was . . . I was hired late in the game. It's a '30s Texas piece, and it was set in prison, and I knew exactly what needed to happen to it, and I jumped in to start to do the rewrite. Almost immediately the seven women in this women-in-prison movie in Texas conspired against me, because they all sounded exactly alike, and I realized I was going to be essentially working for minimum wage on this because there were going to be many, many, many hours spent trying to . . . You can't just go, "Oh, I'll give this one this accent and this one . . ." You have to go back to the start and to the very, very middle of the characters and try to differentiate them.

Drawing a character is like drawing dialogue in that sometimes . . . You know how you'll describe a friend of yours, and you could list his resume, and that's really not emblematic in any way of who that person is, but if you go, "I'll tell you the kind of person Bob is. Bob's the kind of guy that . . ." and that one sentence kind of sums Bob up. In some way that's your touchstone to a character, and that also can be a touchstone to dialogue too sometimes.

AUGUST: There are two kinds of structure you can confuse. There's the overall structure of your movie, which is how the whole story plays out, but there's also the structure of the scene, and dialogue really comes down to the scene work—where you're entering the scene, what's happening in the scene, and where you are getting out of the scene. A lot of times you have trouble with dialogue because you're starting the conversation too early. If you come to the scene a little later and get right to the meat of it, you can be better off. Or maybe you're not finding the right way out of the scene.

A lot of my process for figuring out the scene is just closing my eyes and looping the scene over and over and over and over in my head to figure out what happens in the scene and starting to listen to who's talking and what they're saying. You figure out what the needs are, what you know, and what needs to be said by your characters. Sometimes that takes forever. It's really easy to write the five-page version of the scene, but you know the scene needs to be a page, so your challenge as a writer is to figure out how to distill that down so everyone is saying just what he needs to say, yet it still feels natural. That's why it can take all day to write one short scene. There are scenes that are really easy, where it just flows really naturally, and there are times when just getting those pieces of dialogue to fit right is your day's work.

When I first started writing screenplays, I was more in love with my dialogue than I was with the script in total. I used to think of it almost like a stage play, and the dialogue had such importance to me—"Isn't this clever?" and "Isn't this great?" I'm not saying it's not important to me now, but I'd love to write a script that had no dialogue in it. It would be fantastic. If it has the moments . . . Essentially that's what writing a film or making a film is—a series of moments.

It's not an active process for me anymore, but I've always been very observant. I've always been the guy that sits at the edge of the room, who listens and watches to see how people are doing their things and what they're saying or what they're doing—that sort of psychiatrist aspect of screenwriting. Dialogue is what people would really say if they had an extra ten or fifteen seconds between interchanges; it's just slightly optimized. You're taking out the false starts, the little things that wouldn't matter, that aren't really necessary. If you could listen to a transcript of yourself talking with somebody and then make that a little bit tighter, that's dialogue. It's just a little bit better than how people actually speak.

It also varies by genre. There are certain genres where you do get away with people saying outrageously complicated things they couldn't really say in real life the same way you have movies where things can fly and where cars blow up when you touch them, that's just the nature of the world. There are levels of style to dialogue too. Sometimes knowing what kind of movie you're making is greatly affecting the dialogue, and your dialogue is greatly affecting what kind of movie it feels like. "Hard-boiled detective" has its own expectations. *Lord of the Rings* doesn't have realistic dialogue in any way, but the dialogue is appropriate for the nature of that movie.

People should never introduce themselves. The audience needs to know who those people are, but you can almost always get around someone having to say who they are. And you can usually get out of the scene before people need to say goodbye. A lot of times in a script, one character will tell another character what just happened; you can almost always get rid of that. There are moments that would happen in real life that don't happen in movies, because they're not cinematic or they don't provide new information. You're always looking for what the characters need to say to each other, but also what the audience needs to know in order to advance their understanding of the story and the characters.

HANCOCK: It's a really good point. Sometimes the solution comes from figuring a way into the scene or asking if the scene is beginning or ending at the wrong place, and that can be the solution for writing good dialogue. I remember writing for the stage and writing plays, you would have to have the person come in and introduce himself. In movies it's great because you start in the middle and end before the end, and that can be helpful not only in making things more brief, but also you have to look at a script or movie as kind of a compact with an audience, an interactive experience, so the dialogue can't be or shouldn't be something that lays everything out. There should be the interplay. I'm filling in gaps because I want you to be thinking with me, so the role of the character in the piece is very specific in that way.

AUGUST: There can be a lot of pressure in a scene when you know exactly what needs to happen, so I'll often just take the two characters and have them talk about whatever. You can still hear those characters talking and differentiate their voices. If that scene goes on for seven pages, that's fine. It's just a writing exercise. That has been helpful for me figuring out the difference between two characters who could otherwise be very much the same. Sometimes there are little snippets of what I'm doing in that exercise that will make it into the movie, but it's really just a helpful way of hearing the difference between the characters in my head.

HANCOCK: It's a great thing to do.

AUGUST: When I directed my first movie, I noticed there's this weird handoff that happens between the writer and the actor, which doesn't really go through the director. As the writer, I was each of the characters in the movie. Then, one by one, they got assigned to actual professional actors. I have my performance for all those characters in my head, and the actors have theirs. It's just different, and they have different voices and different ways of doing things.

There have been times in the past where I've needed to rewrite lines because an actor couldn't say them. I always got really frustrated—"Why are you . . .? You're supposed to be a talented actor. You should be able to say this line." And you realize that if it doesn't make sense in their heads, if it doesn't make sense coming out of their mouths, it's just a worthless line. You can't fight to protect those things. It's not going to make it in the movie if you're trying to hold on to your line versus the line they could actually say. All this discussion about the best dialogue, it all ultimately depends on the person who's saying it. So recognize that down the road in this process you may need to change lines simply because of the person that's going to end up saying them.

HANCOCK: That's an interesting point, because one of the great things about directing something that you've written . . . It's amazing how 90% of the time on the set, when something's not coming out of someone's mouth correctly or it just doesn't hit your ear right, you'll just jettison it. There will be that one thing that nobody else thinks is important that you'll go, "No, you have to keep that word in. You keep dropping that word. It's really important." And so it's that one thing that you'll hang on to, and the other you'll go, "I don't care. You can say it the other way."

AUGUST: I have a lot of sympathy for any actor working for a writer-director because we definitely have specific ways of saying things. It's like, "You know what? That was fantastic. You know what would be even better? If you said the line the way it was written."

A lot of times actors are not deliberately changing things; a line just works differently in their heads. On *Go*, for example, we shot it entirely at night, and we were all exhausted. I always have my ComTac earphones on, and we have these little portable TV transmitters, but I would run to the bathroom or something when they're shooting the grocery store, and I was coming back, I'm listening on the ComTacs, and all of a sudden it's, "Oh, crap, he changed the line."

They were so tired, shooting covers on two sides, and they didn't realize they changed the line over the course of eight takes, and so now the two sides didn't make sense. They didn't track with each other and our script supervisor wasn't the kind of person who would interject herself to point that out, so we had to go back and turn around the cameras. You couldn't cut the two sides together because the lines wouldn't fit. They changed a "his" to a "they," or whatever. That's why a writer is actually a helpful person on set sometimes.

Big Fish has multiple conflicting voiceovers in it. In the opening set piece there's a bit by Will, who's kind of my surrogate in the movie, who says, "My father and I were like strangers who knew each other very well." Writing that was the key to understanding what the movie was about. That's the dynamic of this relationship, and without that piece of dialogue . . . You could probably take that piece of dialogue out of the movie and the movie would still make sense, but without that piece of dialogue I couldn't have written the movie. That was the key to that dynamic. It wasn't that they hated each other; it's just that they fundamentally didn't understand each other.

There was a scene that got jettisoned from the movie, but really sprung from that line. Sandra (Jessica Lange) is in the supermarket, and she tells Will that it's a wonder parents and kids can stand each other at all. She says, "Throughout your entire life you're going to pick who you're going to associate with. You pick your friends. You pick the person you're going to love. But with parents and kids it's just a lottery, just like numbers drawn out of a dark bag." There's all this pressure and expectation that you should have this magical relationship, but you didn't choose each other. That all sprung from that one line, which was during my initial discovery process on the movie.

HANCOCK: I don't know if it's an example of good dialogue or bad dialogue, but it's dialogue that I like—when I came in and did a rewrite on *The Alamo*, there was a relationship in the movie between Travis and Bowie, which is there always. These guys go at each other nonstop, and there's a scene toward the end of the movie or toward the end of their relationship where it's obvious that things are going to end badly. Bowie's probably going to die, and Travis is probably going to die as well, and there's this one moment where they actually kind of come to terms with one another and their differences.

I don't think it's an overwritten scene at all, which is nice, and at the end of the scene Travis is leaving, and Bowie says, "Buck, did it matter?"

Travis just looks at him and says, "I'll fetch you some water," or something.

People ask what that means, and I tell them I think it means something to me, but I think it can mean several things. Then people ask if he's talking about some kind of a religious thing, and I tell them I don't know, but it could be. Maybe he's talking about the fact that they are fighting for Texas, and did it matter? I don't know. Is it too ironic? I don't know. I always liked the line, so when it was in the movie, I had people from Disney ask what it means and tell me that it was confusing. I told them I just liked it. I don't know if it's good dialogue, bad dialogue, or whatever, but I liked it because there could be many interpretations, and I think it was true to the characters. It didn't seem out of the way at all.

AUGUST: You feel so powerful when you actually start having characters talk to each other. Your first scripts become a lot of, "Wow, I can have these characters talk to each other, and they can make references to things, and they can say the things I would never say!" That feeling is so giddy and powerful, but that's not generally a helpful way to make a movie or write a script.

You have to really look at the story you want to tell. How does it break down into individual moments? Don't think about those as dialogue moments. What are the turns and twists and changes in the story? You come down to, "Okay, I know I'm writing the scene in which this character discovers that his wife is having the affair with the dog walker. This is the moment where he does this." It is only when you're down to that small moment that you are looking at, "Well, how does that come out in this dialogue? What are those moments?"

Rather than trying to write those lines ahead of time, I want to look at it like, "This is the moment, and inside this moment I'm just playing through this scene. What are the things that could happen? What would be said, and what is the best way into that?" There is this instinct to stare at the screen and think, "Okay, he said this. Now she's going to say that."

But rather than "this character talks, and then this character talks, and then this character needs to talk," you're better off figuring out everything that's being said in the scene, and then arranging it.

HANCOCK: I had an early lesson in what dialogue is supposed to be and how it serves at the pleasure of the script in some ways. I directed a movie that was a straight-to-video movie in the early '90s, and thankfully no one can ever find it, but it was one of those horrible exercises where almost every day the producer would come and say, "We lost the location today." We were just getting set up. Where were we going to shoot the scene? You'd find yourself going to the day's work and trying in your mind to figure out, "How am I going to make this story make sense?"

The only way I was able to do it was to give additional lines to people in other scenes, and so the scenes would become ridiculous exercises like daytime soaps—"Remember last week when Bob left Alice?" and that kind of stuff. I actually learned a lot about what dialogue is not supposed to be, and sometimes that's more important than understanding exactly what it is supposed to be.

Conversing with Your Characters

AUGUST: It's all interior monologue for me. I'm not saying that stuff out loud, because if I hear my own voice then I'm not hearing their voices.

I'm not always necessarily hearing exactly the words they're saying. I have my scribble scene, which is basically just the flow of the conversation. I'm going to go back through and fix those words, but I know what the points are they're trying to get across.

I have a full-length mirror in our dressing room, and there have been times where I'll just sit in front of that mirror and . . . I won't talk through the scene, but I'll sort of see it through. A lot of good dialogue isn't just the words you're saying, but it's the punctuation. It's the starts and the stops, and where people interrupt each other. You can get a feel for it by play-acting the scene a little bit. It's not just what they're saying, it's how they're saying it and what they're not saying or what got cut off before they finished the thought.

HANCOCK: I'm more interested in behavior than I am dialogue, and I think sometimes if the dialogue can support behavior . . . It's not so much for me that I have a conversation with them as I can put them in a million different circumstances outside the specific circumstances of this story and know how they'll behave. That's a great feeling, because then they live for you. They're not just at your service for this script.

There's a lot of really smart people that have talked about how we watch movies, the fact that it's 24 frames per second, how we blink, how we watch, and how it puts us in a dreamlike trance. I think in some ways a script should do that as well, and I think there's a visual component to reading a script. It's not just a story. The worst-case example would be, you get the script, and it's all text, or the dialogue goes on forever. Find a way to break up dialogue where it works on the page. I think you want your eyes to dance on the page, and I think you want to be light on your feet where you need to be light on your feet with the script. If you've got somebody that has a long speech, I think you have to be really creative in ways to break that up to help the audience understand that this is of import and to essentially underline the things that are important.

AUGUST: In terms of the flow on the page or the feel of the page, I try not to put more than four lines of action together in a paragraph. It becomes too daunting to read. When you're reading a dialogue block, if it goes on for more than five or six lines, it gives you the sense that it must be a major speech. You get one or two of those in a script, where it could be half a page; one character's talking, and there is a giant exclamation point, because it's clearly an important speech.

Other times you have something breaking up that big block of text. If it's a character that needs to say quite a few things back to back, find some change in the scene that gives you an excuse to break in with a line of action.

When you have two characters talking, you realize as you read that you stop paying attention to the characters' names. At a certain point you're just reading the dialogue, and even then lines of action are easy to use to break it up. People might not actually really read those, but they're there to sort of give a sense of the scene's flow.

You say people are only reading the dialogue, but your actors are only reading their own dialogue. If you have a table reading before you go into production, it gives the actors a chance to give you notes about lines they have a hard time saying, but it's really just so they can sit down and read the entire script. They will not have read the entire script unless you've actually sat them down in a room with all the other actors and made them go through it. Then they understand that the line they're saying actually refers to something that happened.

You're not trying to handicap your actors and directors with, "Oh, he had to turn at this moment," but you're trying to get them to understand that it's literally a turn of the scene. Sometimes you have to do that, because otherwise you're going to miss crucial points. If you don't break that line out, they're going to steamroll though it and not get that it actually happened.

I notice in looking through older scripts that we have changed the way we put words on the page. Scripts now read a lot more like how movies are actually shot. We use more scene description in movies than we used to, and our dialogue is broken up more. I think screenwriting has morphed into this thing where it has to really feel like the final movie—like you watched the movie by reading the script. The key terms are part of that, building the whole scene even if the director isn't choosing to do it that way. You're giving the spiel for what the whole scene is.

HANCOCK: It's less a piece of literature and more a blueprint for what it will become. Early in my career I'd write this beautiful piece of description about someone's apartment or something, and you'd say it belongs in a book, not in a screenplay. There's the famous example—I'm not sure who it was. It may have been Joe Eszterhas—"Interior, Bob's Apartment, Night, Shitty."

Then there's the other one—"Interior, Bar, Night. This place is every joint Joe Friday ever walked into." Immediately I see the red booths and the cocktail waitress who spent way too many years there. It's an interactive experience for the reader. You're trusting the writer's imagination. You come to the party with your ideas.

AUGUST: But I find if that scene were early in the script, it would probably have a little more description. There's a pacing to how you're doing scene description over the course of the movie. The new location you're introducing quite late in the movie doesn't get that same love, not just because you're tired, but also because you've got to get done.

HANCOCK: When you're reading a script, you know very quickly if you're in the hands of someone who's a good storyteller, or at least someone you want to tell you a story. I think when you sit down to write either a script or a story, sometimes you're telling a story to someone, and then sometimes you're putting your arm around them and telling the story, and there are varying degrees of distance you keep from the reader. I think one of the best at putting his arm around you and telling you a tale is William Goldman. He has that ability to go outside the script and outside the movie and say, "Didn't I just tell you this? Weren't you paying attention?" That's the kind of stuff that, if I were to try it, it would be really, really pretentious and wouldn't work, but for some reason, in the best of his stuff he had the ability to put his arm around you and sit by the fire and tell you a tale. When people try to emulate that, sometimes it pisses me off.

AUGUST: You will find your style. I'm a "we" person, so there's "we" in the script—that hand around you saying, "We see this," or "We feel this," which is just a surrogate for the camera and the audience. I always try to write a script as if you're sitting in the seat watching and experiencing it at the same time you're reading the words, but that's a style thing. I think you don't discover what your style is until you're a couple of scripts in.

Introducing Characters

AUGUST: "The second prettiest girl in Topeka." Her dialogue could be fantastic, but what you gave us with, "Twenty-two, Attractive," means we're not reading her lines with any sort of charge. We have no spin coming into it, so we're not anticipating this is going to work out great.

I always come to—you're not writing a screenplay, you're writing a movie. That's your final product. You have to be able to sacrifice some of your literary intentions. In screenplays you're really limited to what you can see and what you can hear, and if you can't get to something through one of those two senses, you're going to have to write a book.

Dialogue and Reality

HANCOCK: What is dialogue? Is it real? Of course it's not. It's hyper-realized real. You know that, but I've been thinking a lot lately about how unrealistic dialogue is in another way. I think this is particularly important during a political season. How many lies do we tell a day? I mean half-truths really, and not in a malicious way. I'm just saying we kind of reveal ourselves through the lies we tell. How many do I tell a day, 50, 100? I don't know. Somebody says, "How are you doing?" and I just say I'm doing fine. That's not really . . . There are little ones and big ones.

I'm not sure if that matters, but I started thinking about it in terms of screenplays and wondering how my characters can reveal themselves through the lies they tell. It seems like in screenplays is the only time. People pretty much . . . If they're lying, you know it. They always state their intentions fairly clearly. It's just a question, is that important to do? How hard is it to do? Is it just part and parcel of writing good dialogue? I don't know.

AUGUST: A lot of times when you have two characters talking—a husband and wife talking—it's not that what they're saying isn't important, but really what you're watching is the interaction between those two. They could be talking about how the cat needs to go to the vet, but how you're shaping that scene is going to tell us the nature of their relationship, how truthful they're being, what's really going on, and the subtext of what's happening. "Subtext" is one of those dangerous words because you don't just layer up your dialogue with more subtext. That's generally not the goal. The goal is to tell your scene, but your subtext is why this moment is happening, and the way it's happening between these two characters.

Hopefully everyone has something that shoots, and you get to see actors do your lines, but I know John Lee has done TV, and the amazing thing when you're casting a TV show is that you bring in these actors who are auditioning for your parts, and you might see 100 actors for a role, and they're only reading these two scenes that you've written for this process. You realize how completely different your lines sound from certain actors versus other actors. You want to kill yourself at certain points because you can't believe how bad it is, and then you find that one actor who's saying exactly the same things as the other ten guys, but you really believe it coming from him.

If a movie gets a bad review, nine times out of ten the screenwriter is mentioned, and if a movie gets a great review, one time out of ten the screenwriter gets mentioned. If a movie isn't working, they hear the dialogue. They hear everything, and everything grates, or it wasn't well cast, or it wasn't well directed. The process of casting is realizing how crucial it is to get the right people to say those lines.

I have a project now which starts shooting in July, and there are talented people involved in it, so I'm sure they're going to find the right actors, and yet I do have my little list that I sort of slip under the door, hoping that at least some of these people are going to say some of these lines.

HANCOCK: The reason why "Forget it, Jake. It's Chinatown" is a great line is because it kind of codifies the whole theme of the movie. It's an example of where dialogue has to carry the water at the end of the day so people understand what the movie's about. That's essentially what the movie's been about.

I think in terms of starting a movie, more now than ever, I really, really want to please. I look at those first five pages and ask, "Am I excited to read this?" It's not just because I'm a seller in a marketplace. It's because I want to keep myself from being bored to tears. I want to be excited working on it. A lot of times when I'm starting something from scratch, whether it's an original or adaptation, I'll start too early in the rewrite. Many people have said that all problems are first-act problems, but I'll go back and know I can start later, and that goes to a scene, too, in terms of the structure of a scene. You can really goose something and make it something you want to read.

AUGUST: I'm trying to think through my movies and figure out what the last lines are, and most of them I couldn't tell you. The last moment of the movie is a visual moment. It's a resolution of something, but it's not the line. "So what are we doing for New Year's?" was a good summation of, "You know, a bunch of shit happened, and you pick yourself up and dust yourself off, and you just go to it again." But most of my movies, I wasn't writing to a line. I was writing to a conclusion. I was writing to the last thing that happens that closes this movie, but not what people said.

When characters are being shrouded—when characters are acting in the movie—we need to know enough about who those people are independent of what's going on, and you need to give us as an audience a sense that what this person's saying isn't entirely true. The next movie that's shooting is *Dark Shadows*, and one of the characters introduces herself as someone completely different than who she is, and so I can tell the audience not to trust her. I'm setting up scenes in a certain way so you're always really suspicious of everything she says, and that's going to be the case with you too. Or if you have two characters who are changing roles, as long as we heard their voices clearly at the start, it's going to be okay. We're going to be able to work with you. Make sure they have very different names so we don't get confused. Never name two characters with the same first letter. Don't have a Charlie and a Chris in the same movie because you're going to get those people confused. Charlie and Raul, you won't get those confused.

Creating Character Manifestos

AUGUST: I tend to write character introduction lines in a script first. The process of distilling down who this person is to just two sentences is so hard that it makes me think through a lot. I just did a web-video project called *The Remnants*, and had to figure out who the six characters that carry over the whole series were going to be and distill those down to those little short introductions. I literally did combine a couple of different characters and realized—rather than the white survivalist guy, what if it was a black marketing guy? I can put these two guys together, and it's more interesting to merge them and distill them down to core elements.

HANCOCK: Early in my career I did one of those manifestos, if you want to call it that, and it ended up being really, really boring. I couldn't read it, because I think it ended up being more like a resume in some ways. A person isn't his or her resume. They're usually far more interesting than that, so I think how you reveal your character—whether it's through the lies they tell, or whether it's by putting them in some kind of a scene or behavior that throws them at an audience—also can reveal to you, the writer, who they are.

The first time you see a character, before they say a word, you should be speaking to the audience about what kind of person this is, just the first visual of the person. I think what John is saying is that the first description of the character . . . Is he in the corner sitting by himself mumbling? Well, that says something right there. We don't even hear the words, but . . . Yeah, no manifestos for me, but I think the idea is a good one.

6

Rewriting

I was told that if you get stuck, you just have to keep writing. It doesn't matter what you write. Just grab one of the great scripts, whether it's *The Big Chill*, *Chinatown*, or *Schindler's List*, and start writing. Just copy it out. I actually did this while I was at film school. I grabbed *Chinatown*, and about the time when Jake decides to give Curly the cheaper bourbon, I had an idea for my script. I don't know why, but when you're actually writing the words of the great writers, somehow you can be connected to energy that can break you out of your thing. It was really useful. ★ SACHA GERVASI (director of *Hitchcock*, writer of *The Terminal*)

Writer's Block

A Conversation with Bud Shrake
and Bill Wittliff

What to Do When You Get Stuck

BILL WITTLIFF: I find sometimes that if I get jammed on a scene, it's good to take the scene and turn it absolutely upside down. If he says, "Darling, I love you, and I want to marry you," I'd turn it completely over and have him say, "You bitch, I really hate you. I don't want to see you again." Sometimes, that really is the answer. I kept trying to make this work, and the answer was, it was exactly the other side of the coin.

I'm not a thoughtful writer. I don't try to think anything through. I'm not recommending this, but it's strictly feel for me. If it feels right, I go with it. I get in trouble when I think. I don't recommend that, because if you think your way through a script and you get in trouble, generally speaking you can go back through your chain of thoughts and figure out where you went awry. If you do a script strictly on feel and you run into trouble, generally there is not a chain that you can track. You just have to walk around for a few weeks and pray.

BUD SHRAKE: In an earlier life I wrote literally thousands of newspaper columns and magazine stories, and all of them on deadline. Of course, there were many days when I would sit down, and my mind would be a total blank, and maybe I had an hour to go before I had to turn in this newspaper column for the *Dallas Morning News* or somebody. One thing I learned—a very practical thing to do was to write the next line. Forget the big picture, and just write the next line and then the next line after that. Pretty soon things would open up, and I would know where I was going.

I found that works also in writing novels or in writing screenplays. If I'm stuck, I forget about the big picture and forget how this is going to look to eternity and just write the very next line. What does this character say next?

Figuring Out Your Characters

WITTLIFF: Occasionally a character will just stop dead on you. They won't talk, and yet when they first hit the paper it seemed like you knew them absolutely. You didn't have to push them to say anything. Then all of a sudden, they stop talking. They're alive one second, and then in the next second they won't talk to you. And now they're willing to talk again.

So I did this little thing where I would take them out of the script, I would get other sheets of paper, I would stick them in a Corvette, I would stop at a 7-Eleven, I'd have them buy a couple of six-packs of Lone Star, and I'd cut them loose. I'd put them on a Hill Country road, and they'd be doing 60 miles an hour, 70 miles an hour, 80, 90, off the road, and dead. Then I would take them to the pearly gate, and St. Peter's there, and he's got a little checklist. He'd say, "Who are you?"

"Bob Watkins. I was killed back there on the Hill Country road. I'm coming in."

"No, you're not. In 1962 you did so and so."

Basically, what I'm saying is, put them in a situation where they have to explain themselves because their alternatives are heaven or hell. It is amazing. It's also fun to do. It's amazing how they will cut loose sometimes and start talking. Before long you know that character better than you ever thought possible—other facets of them—and it just illuminates the whole thing. And it's enormous fun. Little tricks can get them out of the script and into a place where you can get to know them so that when you put them back in the script they're not shadowy figures to you. And now they're willing to talk again.

Everybody's got little games they play to keep writing. The whole deal really is, writers write. When it's good, they're glad and they keep writing. When it's bad, they wad it up and throw it away and keep writing. We can talk all day and all night, but that's what it comes to—writers write. You don't have to know six scenes down the track. You just have to write the next sentence. That next sentence will tell you whether it's going right or not, and if it isn't, get yourself another sentence.

The Writing Process

SHRAKE: I forget who it was that said it's like traveling across the country at night. You turn on your headlights, and your headlights will only illuminate the first hundred yards of the road, but you can get all the way across the country that way, a hundred yards at a time.

WITTLIFF: Let me tell you something else I believe. It is simply not possible to have an itch without the ability to scratch. If you put something on paper that has not yet resolved itself, you nevertheless have the resolution somewhere in you or you wouldn't have been able to put the question on the paper. I believe that's a great gift we all have—you cannot itch without the ability to scratch.

When I started, my wife and I had a small regional book publishing company, and I really got involved in writing. I found I was taking so much time away from my family at that time . . . We had one child. I started getting up one hour earlier, and that hour . . . I'd get coffee and cigarettes, my notebook paper, and my pencil. That hour was mine, and I was very consistent. One hour every morning, every day, every week, every month. It is astonishing how much work you can get done in one hour a day that's not interrupted or where you don't feel guilty about taking it away from family or business or whatever. It was just a deal I made with myself—I'm taking this hour out of my sleep. This is my hour, and here's how I'm spending it. Writers write. You're not going to be inspired if you're not sitting there with your paper.

I find that a lot of times I'm reaching for more than I can grasp. I'm simply not man enough to get hold of what I'm reaching for. It is really hard to come to a point and say, "I'm just not mature enough for that." Maybe next year, maybe in a couple of years. You never lose that stuff. Nothing's ever lost. Scripts that fail, bodies that are all over the floor in your writing room, they spring back to life a year later or something. "God, I need a redheaded woman, and there she is. She died in 1982, but now she lives again." They're all real.

What works for you? That really is the question. What works for you? You're not going to have an answer for me, and I'm not going to have an answer for you. You just say, "I'm jammed on this. What works for me?" If you can state it just that simply, you will absolutely find a way around it. You simply cannot have an itch without the ability to scratch. The trick is recognizing it when it pops up in front of you. And it will.

Again, this business of wanting to look good . . . It's the wrong question to ask when you're writing. It's a perfectly legitimate question after you've written, but while you're writing it's just simply the wrong question. At least, it's what jams me.

The best we have is who we are and what we've got. I'm not any good at all at doing somebody else's version of something. If it's going to have any worth to me at all, I have to make it mine. That doesn't mean it's going to be good, but at least you find some other part of yourself that you didn't know about before by taking somebody else's character and reinventing it to accommodate who you are both as a person and as a writer.

Tales from the Trenches

WITTLIFF: It's like Mark Twain said—"When I was a boy of 14, my father was so ignorant I could hardly stand to have the old man around. But when I got to be 21, I was astonished at how much the old man had learned. . . ."

Bud, tell that story about the guy who gave all the notes. You remember that?

SHRAKE: No. You tell it.

WITTLIFF: Well, I'll make it my story if I can remember it. Ask me to tell that story.

SHRAKE: Tell that story, Bill.

WITTLIFF: There was a writer. I think it was Bud. At the time, there was this very famous director, and Bud sent him a script. The director read the script, he liked the script, they had a meeting, and the director said, "Get out your notepad," so Bud did. Then the director said, "Do this, do that with this script." So for a day and a half they talked notes. Bud went home, and for six weeks he did all those things. He came back to the director, the director read it, and he said, "This is fucking awful, and nobody would ever make it."

Bud said, "I did everything you said to do."

Then the director said, "That's the problem."

SHRAKE: Yeah, I remember that now.

WITTLIFF: There was a script . . . I can't remember which one it was. An actor and a director got involved. This was early in my career. They liked it, but there was a little of this, a little of that, that needed work, so I did another draft, and they said it was pretty good, but there was still a little of this, a little of that, and I said okay. And I'm doing these for free, which in this business really makes you look like an amateur. The worst thing you can do once you get a deal going somewhere is to offer to do something for free, because they think that's what it's worth. It's worth nothing.

So I did maybe four drafts of this script. Then these two guys came down, and we're going to Mexico because part of the story takes place there, and I'm taking them down there to show them some stuff. The actor says, "I know what. The script needs blah-blah-blah . . ."

I said, "That's in the first draft."

The director says, "Here's what we do . . . blah-blah-blah . . ."

I said, "That's in the third draft." And they're quiet. So we go through maybe four suggestions, and I realize they hadn't read all the drafts. And I said, "You sorry bastards. You didn't even read the three other drafts," and they had not. That's hard to deal with.

These are all funny stories, but this is hard duty. It's hard to be treated so casually and be read so thinly. But, again, we're in the Mafia and this is the life we chose.

SHRAKE: I have to tell one of my favorite stories about dealing with directors. I was working on *Tom Horn*. The director at the time was Elliot Silverstein, who had just directed *Cat Ballou*, which had won a couple of Academy Awards. Elliot thought he was really hot stuff. I go into his office one day, and he says, "I've got a really great idea for a scene. It starts off with Tom Horn standing at the window, and Geronimo is standing there, and Tom says, 'Da, da, da, da, da.' Then Geronimo says, 'Duh.' And then Tom says, 'Da, da, da, da, da.' Then Geronimo says, 'Duh, duh, duh, duh, duh.'" Then Elliot says, "You're not getting this down."

I said, "Getting what down?"

And he said, "Look, I've got this scene in my mind. I dreamed about it last night. I can see the scene perfectly, and I'm giving you the rhythm of it, the rhythm of how this scene plays."

So I said, "But what's the, 'Da, da, da, da, da'?"

Elliot said, "Well, those are the words. You're the writer. The words belong to you."

Anyway, Elliot got fired that afternoon.

As far as writing goes, I kind of do the same thing. I keep going in, and if I don't write anything, I go home, and I come back the next day and do it again. I know that's a common problem. It's a common problem we all have. I've found no solution to it. ★ STEVEN ZAILLIAN (*Gangs of New York, Schindler's List*)

Bill Wittliff on When to Let Something Go

Don't whip a poor horse until it's absolutely dead. Maybe you ought to move on if you're tired of it. It's not delivering what you'd hoped for. This feels better.

For all of us, there are dead bodies all over the rooms where we write. There are characters that didn't work. And we finally say, "Okay. Move on." Maybe the purpose of a particular script is to move you a little further along, and you learn something. Maybe you can use it in something else later on. These are not religious objects. You can take them over here and set them down for a while.

Also, maybe something in a script really doesn't belong in that script but does belong in the third one down the line. I find that true all the time. These bodies do resurrect sometimes.

Steven Zaillian on
Defining Scenes

What to Keep In, What to Leave Out

Audiences can tell you that. When you preview your film, the hard truth is revealed. You can't hold on to that moment that turns out not to be the special moment. I think that everything I write, I know where the important moments are, and I know which moments are there to get me to the next important moment. I find especially when somebody else directs the film, and even when I do, sometimes it's the in-between scenes that actually come alive and become the important moments. I think there are signposts that we all think we need in the film and consider important because without them we don't have a story, but the magic moments or the things people remember oftentimes aren't those big scenes. Those are the foundation scenes. Those are the signposts.

Anne Rapp on Keeping
the Writing Fresh

Most of the time the rewriting is the fun part. The hard part is getting something on the page the first time around. Sometimes when you are rewriting and you don't feel you are making your story any better, it can be agonizing.

The hardest part for me is to keep it fresh. I don't know how many times I've written scenes and then put the script away for a while, and when I go back and read it, it feels so much better, even though there was something missing the first time. I don't necessarily make it better. I make it different. That's the ongoing problem: making something different, not necessarily making something better. I think that's when you really need to listen to somebody else's point of view. You have to have confidence in what you have done but also to not be afraid to listen to someone else's ideas.

I've heard Bill Wittliff say this several times—"Half the time you are in these big Hollywood committee meetings, and the best idea of the day comes from the moron in the corner." You have to be open to listening to the moron in the corner. Very often, the moron in the corner is me.

Nicholas Kazan's
Rewriting Process

Rewriting screenplays is hell, but you have to rewrite almost every screenplay again and again and again. It used to be that I would do a certain amount of preparation and then write my first draft in ten days. Then I'd take two days off and rewrite it in ten days. Then I'd take two more days off and rewrite it again. In 34 days I had something approximating a reasonable first draft. I don't do that anymore because rewriting is such hell. What used to happen to me was that at the end of 34 days I would have characters that worked pretty well, scenes that worked pretty well, and a structure that by and large worked pretty well but had some problems.

Now I delay the point of beginning my first draft as long as I possibly can. I make sure that I've solved every problem that I can discern. You can't see them all, and you have to start writing at a certain point. I have to start writing when my energy reaches a certain level. I just can't prepare anymore. The thing wants to be written. I always say that I've reached critical mass and it has to go down on paper.

Don't Ditch Your First Draft!

Always keep your first draft because your first draft expresses your primal impulse. By writing another screenplay and another, you just improve naturally. When you rewrite, I just encourage you to look at yourself making the changes you make. You have the first screenplay, and if you find five drafts in that you've lost your way, that you don't remember what the screenplay's about, go back and read the first draft, and you'll say, "Oh, yes, now I feel it."

On Rewriting

A Conversation with Daniel Petrie Jr.,
Peter Hedges, and Sacha Gervasi

DANIEL PETRIE JR.: I find that by the time I finish the first draft, I wish I knew when I started what I know now about the characters, so I'm itching to go back. I thought I was kind of hearing their voices when I started out, but now I really hear these characters' voices. I'll go back and really trust that, and go through, and let the characters dictate what the thing is. I'll probably learn many things technically too. Now you have the chance to go back.

PETER HEDGES: I have a friend who's a rewriter, but he does an interesting thing. He'll do seventy drafts in nine days. He'll do a draft where he'll follow one character, the character Joe, and he'll do a draft of Joe. He does these mini-drafts, mini-rewrites. I think sometimes the notion of a rewrite is enormous. I'm actually really learning to enjoy the process. I would like my first drafts to be messier. I've been too careful with my first drafts. I'm now at a point where every assumption I've made about how I write, I'm kind of trying to challenge again to shake it up. Even if it doesn't come to anything, that process, that lone process where it's just you . . . If we can't find some buoyancy, some pleasure in the struggle, in the questioning, in the not knowing, it's bleak. It's hard to get things made, and all of that is true, but if we can nurture a process that is somewhat playful . . . I mean, we're making up things. It's kind of crazy, and it's kind of neat.

SACHA GERVASI: I don't really know what I'm doing until after the first draft. I think it's much harder to go from nothing to something than from something to something better. When I was at film school, the first year I was unable to finish a script. I would get to page 72 and have some sort of emotional breakdown. I'd get drunk and then decide I didn't want to be a screenwriter. For me, it was just about, "Can I get a draft completed?" I'm still figuring it out, but it's a messy individual process.

The most important thing is to just keep moving forward. Sometimes I'm on the third draft, and I realize the movie's actually about *this* person. Sometimes revelations will come in the most unexpected ways, and you'll completely reconfigure your perspective on things. That's the best time, because then you know you're not in control of the process. When it really is working is when I have a sensation that I'm taking notes. It takes around twenty drafts until I've removed myself, and I'm hearing people talk, and I can write it down. To get there is the goal, and it's hard to sometimes.

PETRIE: Sometimes you get notes from friends. Sometimes the notes are valid, and sometimes they're not, but it's always worth listening to when somebody says, "You know what I didn't get?" They may come away thinking the movie is about something you don't think it's about, and that's a real clue to take another look.

Lawrence Kasdan on How You
Know When You're Done

The Coen brothers seem oblivious to all the normal concerns. Their whole careers have been like that and I admire the hell out of them. In *No Country for Old Men*—which I've seen about ten times and think is maybe their best movie—you're with Josh Brolin for the whole movie. He found the money, he's being chased, the killer's after him, and Tommy Lee Jones is after them both. You watch the movie for an hour and forty minutes—Josh Brolin, Josh Brolin, Josh Brolin. Then he gets killed offscreen, and you're not even sure who killed him. Tommy Lee Jones pulls up to a motel, and there's Josh Brolin dead, and we get the idea that the Mexican gang that was tracing them caught up to him and killed him. And then they move on. It does go back to Brolin's wife, but Brolin himself is still offscreen. I can't think of a screenwriting teacher in the world who would say, "Oh, that's how you should do that." It didn't bother me a bit. I love that movie.

No Country for Old Men has that kind of attitude—"This is how Cormac McCarthy told the story, and this is how we're going to tell the story, and if you don't like it, screw you." There has to be that part of you when you finish the thing that says, "This is my story, and I'll stand on that at least until tonight." That's your job.

You never know that you're really done. Instead, you reach a point where you can't do it anymore. You don't know what else to do, so you start showing it to people. Invariably, they've got plenty of ideas. You can choose whether you're going to listen to any of those ideas or not. Sometimes you get defensive about it, and you say, "You guys just don't understand. Wait until you see how I direct it," but in fact, they're right. You don't need this, or you don't need that, or that doesn't work, but it can be hard to be open to it once you've said, "This is my best thought on the matter at the moment." Every step of the way, right through the shooting and right through the cutting, you don't ever feel like, "This is the only way it can be." You feel like, "This is the best thought I have at the moment."

The Magnificent Seven is the Western remake of *Seven Samurai*, and if you haven't seen *Magnificent Seven*, you've got to see that too. It has the coolest cast ever put together—Steve McQueen, James Coburn, Charles Bronson . . . It's absolutely fabulous. There's a scene where Eli Wallach and his group of bandits have taken over the town, and they're having the gunfighters give up their weapons. Eli Wallach says to Steve McQueen, "Why'd you do this? There's no money here. What were you thinking?"

McQueen says, "I asked the same question of my friend who jumped naked into a thistle bush."

Wallach says, "What did he say?"

McQueen says, "It seemed like a good idea at the time."

That's really what creation is about, whether it's writing or directing. You have to trust and go with the best idea you have at the time. If you can stand to look at your movie five years later you may say, "That was not a good idea," but you may think, "That part, that was a really good idea."

7

Collaboration

A Conversation with
Steven Zaillian

MODERATED BY SACHA GERVASI

Beginnings and Inspiration

SACHA GERVASI: Everyone's aware of all the incredible scripts you've written and films you've made, but let's start at the beginning. Was there a particular moment you decided or realized you were going to become a writer?

STEVEN ZAILLIAN: Not really, no. I didn't study writing. It wasn't because I didn't think classes worked. I just didn't really have the opportunity to take any. When I got out of college I kind of stumbled into a job as an assistant film editor. While I was doing that, I met some actors who were in the films I was working on. We decided to try to make a film together. Somebody had to write it. I took a crack at it. I didn't really know what I was doing.

I think it may have been Larry Kasdan who said, "The important thing is to keep writing." You can't really expect your first script to be the one that's going to sell. So I think I wrote three scripts before this fourth one that I'm talking about with these actors. That was the one that did it. I wrote it as a novel because I wasn't too sure, even after having written a couple of screenplays, about the form. My brain didn't really think in terms of screenplay form. I wrote it as a novel but with the idea of it becoming a screenplay at some point. That was *Bad Manners*.

The Writing

GERVASI: You've talked in the past about a fateful trip to Italy in the summer of 1979 or 1980 where you didn't really know what you were doing, but you went off and wrote this novel on the trip. That was sort of a turning-point moment.

ZAILLIAN: It was. It worked out for a number of reasons. I didn't plan on doing it, but I took a trip to Europe, not with the intention of writing and not with the intention of staying. I actually went with one of the actors that I mentioned who was making a movie in Israel. We met somebody on an airplane by chance who was going to Italy. We were stopping over in Italy, and I kind of spontaneously decided to stay. My friend Perry went home and I stayed for about eight weeks.

I rented an apartment, took Italian classes, got the only English-language books I could find at the bookstore, and gradually started writing this script. It was sort of a great way to do it because I was writing about my home, and I wasn't at my home. I couldn't communicate with anybody because my Italian was so bad, and so the writing became a way of communicating and a way to keep my sanity.

In your other panel, you said the best way to start writing is to read good scripts. I agree with that. You take it one step further and actually transcribe the script, and I think that's actually a pretty good idea too.

GERVASI: That is a really good thing. Before I met Steve I was a journalist in England and was reading his scripts. I remember reading them and going, "Oh, my God. It's amazing." Whenever I had writer's block, I would take one of Steve's scripts and begin to type it out. At a certain point, maybe a few pages in, I would suddenly go, "Oh, my gosh," and I would be connected with some wonderful energy. That's something some people may find helpful if they are feeling stuck or blocked. Keep moving. Keep writing.

ZAILLIAN: The other thing you do that I don't but I think is good is, you write other things. You keep a journal. What Sacha does is, he'll get up in the morning, and he'll start writing. He'll start doing the kind of writing where there's not a lot of pressure. You're just writing a kind of diary, and I think that's really helpful too. I've never done it because I'm too lazy, but I do understand how that could be a good thing.

The Falcon and the Snowman

GERVASI: Similarly exciting is when you got the call from John Schlesinger— "Please come up to the house on Sunset Drive, and let's talk about *Falcon and the Snowman*." That must have been a fairly exceptional experience, to be collaborating with one of the greatest directors of the twentieth century.

ZAILLIAN: Well, it just goes to show you how accidental a lot of things are in life. After I sold this first screenplay, which, by the way, was never made, I got hired by producer Edgar Scherick to write another script, an adaptation of the book *Alive*, which eventually was made into a movie, but not with my script. That was fateful for a couple of reasons—not the script itself, or not the work I had done, but because the assistant to this producer was a young guy named Scott Rudin. He was about 18 years old. So I met him at the very beginning, and we've worked together a number of times since then. The other reason was that John Schlesinger had tried to make *Alive* a number of years before, so when someone gave him my script as a writing sample, he was familiar with the project. He was familiar with the book. He could tell what I had done in the adaptation in a way that somebody else who wasn't familiar wouldn't be able to. So having all that knowledge, he liked what I had done.

GERVASI: And how was the experience, being in Mexico on the set with John? Obviously he was incredibly inclusive, which is not necessarily typical. What did that feel like, when your first scene rolled, and you had incredible actors like Sean [Penn] running your lines? How was that experience for you?

ZAILLIAN: I didn't realize how special John was until much later, after I had worked with some other directors. John Schlesinger came from the stage. He came from the English stage. His way of thinking about writers is different from the way Hollywood directors think of them. The writer's a crucial part of the process to him. He likes them. He likes having them around. He likes talking about script. He likes having them on the set. That was very unusual.

The fact that my first script had actors like this in it was very unusual too. Sometimes things have happened in my life that I didn't really realize how special they were until years later, but I knew that this was special.

Early Influences

GERVASI: In terms of moral integrity, I wanted to go back a little bit into your background. Your father was a fairly renowned radio journalist, quite a serious journalist. I wonder, growing up in that household with your dad, what was it like, and to what degree did growing up around that and his values and attitudes inform the way you approach things in your work? It seems there's definitely a parallel between the two of you.

ZAILLIAN: He influenced me in many ways apart from what he did for a living, just in terms of his own kind of morality. In terms of his work, I was always aware that he took it seriously. He was a journalist. My clearest recollection of him working at home, which he didn't do very often, was when he got a job as a radio documentary maker. He would edit the stuff at home, and when I say "edit," I mean cutting quarter-inch tape with a razor blade.

I would hear his documentaries playing over and over as he was working on them. Did it influence me? I don't know. It made me comfortable with the idea of telling real-life stories. It didn't inspire me to be a journalist. I never thought . . . It's interesting to me, and I could see myself doing that now, but at the time I wasn't really interested. I was more interested in things like photography and architecture and things like that.

GERVASI: But you did become an editor.

ZAILLIAN: That's true, yeah, with razor blades.

GERVASI: There is the connection, because what you just described your father doing is what you just described yourself doing.

ZAILLIAN: That's true. A lot of times you see things, and you don't really think about them until later, until somebody points them out on a panel.

The Relationship between Editing and Screenwriting

GERVASI: The relationship between editing and screenwriting, I imagine those skills might be somewhat parallel. What are some of the lessons that might have been applicable from editing a film to writing a script?

It does seem to me, in terms of storytelling, in terms of the way you write . . . What I've observed in some of your scripts is that you get into your scenes as late as possible, and you get out as early as you can. They're incredibly concentrated and focused, those scenes. There's not a lot of fat, and I wonder if that was something that came from editing.

ZAILLIAN: I think it may have, at least a part of it. More than that was to get into the movie as late as possible and get out as soon as possible. Not just in the scene, but in the whole movie. I think that's a mistake a lot of people make. I read these scripts all the time where the writer isn't exactly sure who the character is. They're experimenting with, "Okay, what does the character . . .? Gets up in the morning . . . What does the character do?" They're starting at the very beginning of the day and as far back into the character's life as they need to go in order to understand the character.

At some point in editing I realized that, with most things I was working on, you could take out the first reel, just throw away the first ten minutes, and start the movie where the action starts. That way you'd get to know the character over the course of the real action and not as a kind of preamble. That's something I'm actually very conscious of doing now, thinking about what happens before the story really gets going but not writing it.

The Writing Process

GERVASI: Since you've brought it up, what is your specific process? How long does it take you to write a script? What are the stages? How do you start?

ZAILLIAN: It's really changed over the years. When I was younger I would write much faster. I wrote *Bad Manners* in about six or seven weeks from start to finish. *American Gangster* took eighteen months. You can see there's quite a big difference there. I think the reason for that is that I didn't know as much when I was younger, so I didn't know what I was doing wrong. Now I'm aware of what's bad, or at least I'm nervous about it, so I'm more cautious. I don't think that's necessarily a good thing.

I think the burst of energy where you write really fast can be really good, but my process has become much more deliberate over the years. I work a boring 9-to-5 sort of schedule, going to an office, sitting there. I don't have to write a certain number of pages. I write whatever I can, whatever I can get done.

For the first three months these days, I don't write any script. I just outline on a yellow legal pad. I write notes, ideas, character descriptions . . . I really try to work out the movie all the way through because I'm terrified of getting stuck at some point and saying, "Oh, I'm going to worry about that when the time comes." I would hate to invest six months in something and get up to page 82 and not know what to do.

I can't remember who said—it may have been Hitchcock—that books are written from the beginning to the end, and screenplays should be written from the end to the beginning. The ending of a movie is crucial. I have found this out in my own work, once the movie comes out, and you see an audience's reaction to it. I think the ending is so important that if you don't know the ending when you start, you shouldn't do it.

Schindler's List

GERVASI: I know that so many people are incredible fans of the film, and the script is obviously one of the greatest of all time. Can you talk a little bit about the genesis of that project? Originally it wasn't going to be a

Steven Spielberg film. You were working with Marty Scorsese. Can you talk about when the changeover between Scorsese and Spielberg occurred and what that experience was like?

ZAILLIAN: I got a call from somebody that worked with Scorsese. I'm not even sure how that happened. I know he works with De Niro a lot, and De Niro was in *Awakenings*, so maybe a conversation between them led to me somehow. He was the original director on it, and we worked together on a couple of drafts. It was great. He is somebody who you just sit down with for eight hours and kind of go over the script page by page. Ideas come up, and it's a wonderful kind of experience. In terms of the first draft, he also leaves you totally on your own to do whatever you want. He starts making suggestions after the first draft is done. By the way, Spielberg does the same thing. I think most good directors do the same thing. They leave the writer alone to begin with, and then really get into the process of collaboration on rewrites.

Thomas Keneally had written a very good book, and then I had the good fortune to have access to two of the survivors who are actually characters in the story and who lived in Los Angeles. I talked to them a lot, and they were very enthusiastic about the project. They really wanted to help. They told me their own personal experiences, and I could then extrapolate from that what they were doing on a day-to-day basis both in Krakow and in the camps and kind of what everybody was doing. They were the most important source of research. Then we made a trip to Poland, and that was it.

GERVASI: But at a certain point, Steven Spielberg began working with you. At the time, as you were working with him on the script, did you have any sense of what was going on? I mean, what was your perception of that moment, how did it evolve, and ultimately what was the experience being in Poland?

ZAILLIAN: I think everybody's opinion of it was that this was Spielberg's pet project, but it was never thought of as a commercial project, so there was not a lot of pressure on us to deliver a commercial project. That turned out to be really important. The only thing I wanted was to do it well enough that I didn't look bad. That was my goal. My goal didn't extend beyond the script. I didn't really think in terms of the film.

GERVASI: But the final film is remarkably dutiful to your script. Give or take a couple of things, the reality is that even some of the cuts are in the script. Steven was incredibly faithful to what you wrote, and there's a famous story that at a certain point before he was going to shoot, he sent the script to a couple of esteemed writer friends, including Tom Stoppard. Steven Spielberg sent *Schindler's List* to him, and Tom Stoppard said, "Don't change a single word." I think it was something you were grateful to Stoppard for.

ZAILLIAN: Forever.

I wrote it down because this event in Schindler's life was something he talked about quite a bit. It was kind of a turning point in his life that he recognized. When asked to describe her, he said she was a little girl in a red coat. So that's how we referred to her and how I referred to her in the script. She didn't have a name. She was just the girl in the red coat.

When Spielberg decided to shoot the film in black and white, I said immediately, "But what about the girl in the red coat? Now what? Do we have to give her a name? How is she going to be distinguished?" He made the decision to tint the film. At the time I thought it might be too much. It might take you out of the film. But it didn't. He recognized it as an important enough image that you can do that to it. It was always there, but it became highlighted by his decision to shoot the film in black and white.

★ STEVEN ZAILLIAN (*Gangs of New York, Schindler's List*)

Watching Your Script Brought to Life

GERVASI: What was that experience like? It was such an incredibly horrific event. It must have been a strange sensation to see it brought to life. In one sense, I'm sure it was exhilarating, because there it is coming to life in this incredible story. In another sense, it must have been so real and horrific.

ZAILLIAN: I wasn't there very much. I went to Poland when I was doing research. I was there about a week. We looked around for other places to shoot. I was only there for the first ten days of shooting. The reason was, I was gearing up to do *Searching for Bobby Fischer*, so I had to get back to start on that. Looking back on it, I'm really happy I did that, because when I saw the film, I was seeing it without knowing what it was going to look like. It was a complete surprise to me. I don't think I saw any dailies during the ten days either.

It's a nice experience, and I actually prefer that these days. I very seldom hang out on sets. I did early on, with John and with Penny on *Awakenings*.

EXT. HILLTOP - DAWN

From here, the action down below seems staged, unreal, the
rifle bursts no louder than caps. A man falls to the ground
well before the sound of the shot that killed him arrives.

Dismounting, Schindler moves closer to the edge of the hill,
curious. His attention is drawn to a small distant figure,
all in RED, at the rear of one of the many columns.

EXT. STREET - DAWN

Small red shoes against a forest of gleaming black boots.
A Waffen SS man occasionally corrects the three-year-old's
drift, fraternally it seems, nudging her back in line with
the barrel of his rifle. A volley of shots echoes from up
the street.

EXT. STREET - DAWN

Moving with a long line toward an idling truck, Mrs. Dresner
pulls her daughter into an alcove.

EXT. HILLTOP - DAWN

Schindler watches as the girl in red slowly wanders away
unnoticed by the SS. Against the grays of the buildings and
street she's a bright moving target.

EXT. STREET - DAWN

A truck rumbling down the street obscures her for a moment.
Then she's moving past a pile of bodies, old people executed
in the street, and Pfefferberg prying off a manhole cover -

INT. SEWERS - DAWN

Pfefferberg descends metal rungs into a sewer tunnel. The
noise from above - the dogs and the trucks and orders shouted
through megaphones - echoes weirdly off the walls.

He comes around a corner and sees light - and figures
silhouetted against it - up ahead. They make it to the end of
the tunnel by the banks of the Vistula, but are gunned down by
waiting troops as they emerge. Shielding his head from the
stray bullets ricocheting off the walls, Pfefferberg turns
abruptly back the way he came and runs.

I was there a lot. After that, I just decided my job is really done when I turn in the script. If a director's going to be faithful to it, or whatever they're going to do with it, they're going to do that whether I'm there or not.

I think what Spielberg did was amazing. He brought a kind of visual approach to it that was stunning. You say it's remarkably faithful to the script. It is, but every scene has to be interpreted visually, and he did that with each scene in a really exciting way. The one I remember quite clearly in my original draft is the liquidation of the ghetto, which comes at the end of the first act. I think it was about two pages. He wanted to make it a really big sequence, and it ended up being around fifteen pages. On screen it was about twenty minutes. That gives you an idea of how a good collaboration can work. A good director really brings something to the table you never would have thought of.

Searching for Bobby Fischer and Working with Sydney Pollack

GERVASI: *Bobby Fischer* was a huge experience for you and an incredibly important one. How did that come about, and was the idea of directing something that had been with you for a long time?

ZAILLIAN: It hadn't been with me. Like I said, I didn't call myself a writer for five scripts. I couldn't bring myself to say the words. I would say, "I write, but I'm not a writer. That's what I do for a living." I think most people think writers are writing in order to become directors, and many of them are. It's like a stepping stone to directing. The idea that directing is the epitome of what we can do in this business, I never really felt that way. I really enjoyed writing and the life of a writer. I felt that's what I was good at. I didn't aspire to be a director.

However, I had written a script, and it didn't go well with the director. It was the first time I was involved in something where I sort of locked horns with the director and had to walk away from it. At that point I thought that maybe to protect my work I was going to have to direct something. So it was an example of a bad experience leading to a good one.

I talked to Scott Rudin, who by this time was starting to produce movies. He sent me everything he had that he was interested in, including books, articles, and things like that. One of them was *Searching for Bobby Fischer*, which was this little book with this photograph of this kid on it staring intently at the chessboard. He was about eight years old—Josh

Waitzkin, the chess player—when the book was written. One of my sons was the same age, so I really related to it. In terms of the story, I didn't play chess with my son, but the family story was one I could relate to.

To speak about Sydney Pollack for a moment, he was a great man, a great director, and just a lovely guy to hang out with. I first worked with him because he was the executive producer on *Searching for Bobby Fischer*. The reason he was the executive producer on the film was that I didn't have final cut, but he did even as a producer. Scott didn't have it either. So Sydney came on to protect me, basically. He didn't have a lot to do with the film in terms of the actual day-to-day, but he graciously . . . It was really a favor to us that he came on that film. He did read the script and had one comment, which was a really good one. It was on one line, which I took.

I worked with him two other times. I worked with him as an actor on *A Civil Action*, and again he did that as a favor. He's a brilliant actor. And then I worked with him writing on *The Interpreter*, and that was very intense because they were about to shoot, and I came on about two weeks before they began shooting. I went to New York and worked with him there. There was a lot of talking. It was the only time I worked on a script where I gave pages. I would literally email a page, and he would email it back and say, "What about this?" and it would go back and forth. I've never done that before, but with Sydney it worked out pretty good. It was fun too.

The line in *Searching for Bobby Fischer* that Sydney helped me with is in a scene where Joe Mantegna is talking to Ben Kingsley, really when they first talk to each other in the Backgammon Club, where this kind of smoky tournament is going on, kind of in the beginning of the film. Ben says . . . I think the line is something like, "I'll tell you what I lost when Bobby Fischer disappeared," or something like that. I can't remember exactly what the line is. I actually had an answer for what that was, but Sydney said I shouldn't tell the answer but just pose the question. I thought that was really smart. Again, if you have to come right out and say it, you've gone too far. Posing the question was valid, but giving the answer to the audience wasn't.

GERVASI: *Searching for Bobby Fischer* also began a great collaboration with Connie Hall, the incredible cameraman. What was that like, directing your first film and working with Connie? Was that an experience?

ZAILLIAN: It was my first film, so I was very nervous, and I wasn't sure what a director was supposed to do, and I felt I should be really prepared. I should know everything before I show up, or maybe somebody will ask

INT. HOUSE OF BACKGAMMON - NIGHT

Coke cans, broken glass, soggy candy wrappers and wads of
toilet paper floating in puddles outside the men's room. The
place has cleared out pretty much, the tournament over.

                    FRED
          Clearly you had me come here so I
          could see all this. But if you really
          wanted me to say no to letting my son
          play, you wouldn't have bothered. You
          want me to think you want me to say no
          but you actually want me to say yes.

                    PANDOLFINI
          You have no idea what I want.

Pandolfini sips from a Coke can and surveys the debris all
around them.

                    PANDOLFINI
          What is chess, do you think?
          People who play for fun, or not at
          all, dismiss it as a game. The ones
          who devote their lives to it, for the
          most part, insist it's a science.
          It's neither. Bobby Fischer got
          underneath it like no one before him
          and found at its center - art.
                    (pause)
          I've spent my life trying to play like
          him. Most of these guys have,
          studying every move he ever made. But
          we're like forgers. We're competent
          fakes.
                    (pause)
          Your son isn't. He creates like
          Fischer. He sees like him. Inside.

                    FRED
          You can tell that by watching him play
          some drunks in the [park] -

                    PANDOLFINI
          Yes.
                    (pause)
          You want to know what I want, I'll
          tell you what I want. I want back
          what Bobby Fischer took with him when
          he disappeared. ~~My love of the art of~~
          ~~the game.~~

me a question, and I won't know the answer. I basically storyboarded, on my script, every shot for the movie. Connie Hall doesn't work that way. He'll do it, but he doesn't like it. So he basically retrained me to be more spontaneous.

We would have a rehearsal in the morning, and we would sit and watch it, and then we would discuss together how to shoot it. He said he couldn't even think of how to shoot it until he saw it, and the truth is he didn't even read the script. He read it once, and it was, "Okay." It was a job.

It took about three weeks, and I got totally into his way of working. It's the way I work now. In fact, on *All the King's Men* I was working with another cinematographer because Connie has passed away. Pawel [Edelman] doesn't come from that school. He comes from the school of, "You need to know what you're doing when you get there," so I had to try to retrain him. It was fun.

GERVASI: The film, as everyone knows, came out incredibly well. Shortly after finishing it you were nominated for the Academy Award for your screenplay *Schindler's List* and won. I remember asking you what happened immediately after winning the Academy Award, and you said, "The next morning I went to the office to work." I think that's important to talk about, because being a writer in Hollywood, it's very possible that when success comes, particularly big success, one can be very easily distracted and lose sight of things.

ZAILLIAN: I think it was really the same reaction I described before that having written a script didn't make me a writer. I felt I had to do it more than once in order to become a writer, and I had the same reaction winning an Oscar. It doesn't mean I'm going to win Oscars all the time, so I felt I had to go back to work. I have seen people lose sight of what they're doing and lose their momentum in terms of their work. I have a pretty strict work ethic.

One thing the Oscar did do—one negative thing it did—was it made me feel that whatever the . . . It's like if you're a musician and you have a successful album, you feel like the next one . . . You know, you've got to live up to it. So I turned down a lot of jobs thinking, "Oh, this isn't as good as *Schindler's List*." Looking back on it, I realize that I let certain things go that I shouldn't have, and that that should never be the reason to do something. *Schindler's*, like I mentioned, was a little pet project of Spielberg's. It wasn't meant to be a big film. So you can't plan on these things.

GERVASI: Going to the office and sticking to your routine is really important. I'll briefly share a story. I was at film school at UCLA, and there was a kid in our class who sold a script for a million dollars. He got swept up in the whole thing, and he's now a maître d' in a New York steakhouse. I ran into him recently, and the whole experience of becoming a successful screenwriter while at film school and selling a script for a lot of money, it completely threw him off balance. Keeping your head is a huge part of maintaining a career.

ZAILLIAN: It can go away just as quickly as it happened. That can happen to any artist, and you're not going to know it until it's already happened. You don't see it coming. By the time you find out, it's already happened. Your friend is already working in the steakhouse.

The Writer/Director Relationship

GERVASI: As a writer, when you're working with these types of people—Spielberg, Scorsese, Ridley Scott—do you feel they're bringing out the best in you? Do they challenge you? What's the experience like for you?

ZAILLIAN: A lot of times, the decision I make to work on a film has to do with who else is involved in it. The most important figure is going to be the director. If I have to choose between two things to do and I like the stories equally, the director's going to be the deciding factor. It's crucial.

The thing good directors have in common is that they don't think of themselves as writers, and they actually respect writers. They know how important writers are to them. I feel the same way about them as directors. That kind of mutual appreciation society is very beneficial to a good film. I think that where you get into trouble is where one is not respectful of the other. Mutual respect is crucial, and it comes out of experience from both sides. I think a lot of writers hear horror stories about directors ruining their scripts or taking them away. I've never had that experience with the good ones.

American Gangster and Getting Stuck

GERVASI: *American Gangster* was a painfully long process for you. I think it would be helpful for people to hear, what happens when you get stuck as a writer? How do you get through it when you're sitting there for months, racking your brain going, "How do I make this work?" If Steve Zaillian's stuck, it makes it easier for everyone else.

ZAILLIAN: I was stuck on the outline. I just couldn't see the whole movie, and I felt like . . . As I said before, I can't start until I can see the end, and I couldn't see the end. I went into the office every day for six, seven, eight months and didn't write anything. That had never happened. What kept me going was, I couldn't admit that I couldn't get through it. I felt if I admitted that I couldn't get through it, it would allow me to say that on the next one too. It's like being a compulsive gambler or a drug addict or something. If you do it once, the second time is going to be easier.

By the same token, it was terrifying. I would say things to myself like, "Someday this is going to make a good story. Someday I'm going to look back on this, and it won't be so bad." At the time, it was torture. All I could think of doing was just to keep going back into the room. Finally I had enough confidence to start writing, and then it went very well.

GERVASI: Are there things you know now that you would love to be able to say to your younger self?

ZAILLIAN: In a funny way, it's the opposite. For me, writing is not something that gets easier. For me, writing is actually getting harder, and so I wish my younger self could tell me something to make me work faster. I think there's something to . . . The whole "stay hungry" philosophy is important. Once you get comfortable, it's really hard to keep working.

GERVASI: You said to me once that you didn't want to know too much. You don't want to hear people talk about the themes in your work and the stuff that you've done because if you know too much, you can become conscious, and it's the unconsciousness that makes you free to write what you want. Knowing the rules of screenwriting is a mistake sometimes.

ZAILLIAN: I don't know what the rules of screenwriting are, but if I knew them, maybe I could work faster. It's interesting that there is a real good side to not having done as much as I have. You have a kind of enthusiasm for it that you can't hang on to forever. It's not that I don't like what I'm doing, but I'm so familiar with the job that I'm not surprised as often as I used to be when something good happens.

Peter Hedges on Collaborating

If you want it to be exactly the way you want it to be, write a novel. No one may read it, but you'll have it. The beauty of making films is that this is a business of other people. You surround yourself with people who know more than you who say, "By the way, that idea you have that you think is brilliant, no one gets it," and pretty soon everyone around you is telling you that, and you have an actor like Johnny Depp say, "I don't need to say this line," and you realize he's right. People, life, and the process teach you.

You have to write it so that somebody will give you the money so you can make it, unless you have a lot of money. Then there's the version for the people you're making it with, with the belief that those people are going to align in a common goal to tell a singular story in a way that an audience would enjoy. Then you'll have the great experience of it being shown in front of people, and you start to notice ten minutes in, everybody is shifting in their seats because you lost them. Then you try to figure out why. Then you hope that it's fixable.

Lawrence Kasdan on Writing
with a Partner

The challenge is finding the right person to sit there with and exchange ideas with that makes you happy to be in the room. It's less hard to do the work. You have an appointment rather than an indistinct time when you think you're going to do it. Someone's watching you and it helps in every way—if you like the person and you're not constantly feeling at odds with what they want to do.

I'm very jealous of the Coen brothers, who for all these years have had each other. They've done very unconventional stuff, which I admire, and I think they're more unconventional because they've had each other to say, "Let's just do it. What the hell?" They might not do that alone. That takes unbelievable courage.

I've had collaborators all through my career, and whenever I have, it's been fun, and I've always had those writers come on the set every day. I love them being around through the whole process. I would always prefer to have a collaborator. If I could always do that, I would, but I can't. I can't always find that person.

Randall Wallace on Working
with Other Writers

In *Secretariat*, I did not write the original screenplay. I did work on the script, but a great writer named Mike Rich wrote the original. It was a different experience for me to be starting out with . . . There were some scenes that I just completely wrote from the beginning, but still they were written in the context of someone else's script. They were linked to other scenes. I think that writing a script is like raising a child. There's a way in which you feel absolutely responsible for every tiny thing, and there are other ways in which you have nothing to do with who this person is. They have their own lives.

Mike wrote me a beautiful e-mail when he saw the movie, and I wrote him back and said, "You know, Mike, I want you to know, when you're directing, every decision seems to fall so squarely on the shoulders of the director, that it's easy for the director to start feeling that he or she is the author of every good thought in the movie, and I have prayed that that not be the case with me. And I never have, either in the choice to write a scene or to acknowledge that I've done that, taken away in any sense from the amazing contribution you made." He wrote me back and said, "I will value this note from you as much as I value the words you wrote." I felt that was just an extraordinary thing. If I was ever going to think about doing anything else that somebody else had written, I'd sure look for a Mike Rich screenplay to do that.

John Lee Hancock had done *The Rookie* from a Mike Rich script, and John told me that when he first met Mike, he said, "The good news is, you got a director. The bad news is, you got a director who is a writer." But the great thing about a great writer-director like John is that he recognizes and respects the original writer. The big question the writer-director has—or the big advantage—is to think twice before changing the scene from what somebody else has written. I think a writer-director knows better than a director who doesn't write.

I find that in order to write, I have to learn all of the perils and just let it be. It's like playing with a child. You let them do what they're going to do. You watch them. You leave them alone. They're never out of your heart. So writing this scene and turning it over to another director is . . . In *Braveheart*, I had written that totally about Mel Gibson. I had actually picked him as the person I wanted. But I felt like my father felt on my sister's wedding day when he turned to me and said, "She's got another shoulder to cry on now." It was an insightful and beautiful moment for me, realizing how much my father loved my sister and that he was turning her over to another man to care for her. That's the way I feel about any script someone else is going to direct. When I was writing it, I didn't feel in total control. I felt I had more responsibility to watch what was happening.

When I was working on a script someone else had written, I thought—and I had a great conversation with Mike Rich about this—it's so easy to start thinking that you made it up. When you're directing, every word the actors say, you have to believe it's yours. I've seen it happen many times when directors start to think they actually did write the thing even though the scene is verbatim what the other guy wrote. There's a process of ownership. When it's at its best, it's a union between the script and the direction.

For me, the ultimate thing about being a writer is to write words that are so economical and so focused that they are not changeable. *Braveheart* wasn't exactly verbatim, but it almost was. I know Mel felt he reinvented or had seen within himself, so there's that strange kind of . . . almost like a mother and a father. Both of them look at the child and believe they are totally manifested in that child, and the truth is that they needed each other to do it.

8

Go Forth

I had one really good piece of advice, which is, don't give yourself X number of years in which to make it. There is no timeline. Lots of people I know said, "I will give it three years, and if it hasn't worked out by then, I'll go back to doing whatever I was doing before."

But this friend, the one with the good advice, said to me, "Just be there. No one can kick you out. Just be there. Stand there long enough, and your turn will come around." And it did. It worked out. ★ CAROLINE THOMPSON

I know I get better at rejection. It gets easier somehow. I get more practiced at it. I suffered from that when I first started writing. I was working for Robert Altman, who loved everything I wrote. I thought I must be a genius. Then I had to remember that Altman is one of those directors . . . You can give him a grocery list, and he'll make a movie out of it. Everything to Altman is an outline and a blueprint. Then I got into the real world of movie making. ★ ANNE RAPP

This seems so simple, but you have to keep writing. That means keep writing, keep writing, and keep writing. You may get impatient with how things are going, and you'd be amazed how that filters out most people, because most people don't write even a second script. If you're serious about it, you will somehow be able to keep writing these screenplays when there is very little validation coming from the world. If you can do that, then there's hope. ★ LAWRENCE KASDAN